Super Granny

Super Granny

GREAT STUFF TO DO
WITH YOUR GRANDKIDS

Sally Wendkos Olds

STERLING

New York / London
www.sterlingpublishing.com

STERLING and the distinctive Sterling logo are
registered trademarks of Sterling Publishing Co., Inc.

Library of Congress Cataloging-in-Publication Data

Olds, Sally Wendkos.
Super granny : great stuff to do with your grandkids / Sally Wendkos Olds.
p. cm.
Includes index.
ISBN 978-1-4027-5716-7 (hc-trade cloth: alk. paper)
1. Grandmothers. 2. Grandparent and child. 3. Grandchildren.
4. Creative activities and seat work. I. Title.
HQ759.9.O43 2009
649'.51—dc22   2008031833

2   4   6   8   10   9   7   5   3   1

Published by Sterling Publishing Co., Inc.
387 Park Avenue South, New York, NY 10016
© 2009 by Sally Wendkos Olds
Distributed in Canada by Sterling Publishing
C/o Canadian Manda Group, 165 Dufferin Street
Toronto, Ontario, Canada M6K 3H6
Distributed in the United Kingdom by GMC Distribution Services
Castle Place, 166 High Street, Lewes, East Sussex, England BN7 1XU
Distributed in Australia by Capricorn Link (Australia) Pty. Ltd.
P.O. Box 704, Windsor, NSW 2756, Australia

Sterling ISBN 978-1-4027-5716-7

Book design by Jo Anne Metsch

For information about custom editions, special sales, premium and
corporate purchases, please contact Sterling Special Sales Department
at 800-805-5489 or specialsales@sterlingpublishing.com.

To my Super Grandchildren

Stefan, Maika, Anna, Lisa, and Nina,

My guides on the journey back to childhood,

adolescence, and young adulthood,

Who make the trip lively

And teach me so much along the way

||||||||||||||||||||||||||||||||||||||||||||||

Contents

||||||||||||||||||||||||||||||||||||||||||||||||

The Preschool Years (Ages Three to Six) 47

The School Years (Ages Six to 11)   99

Adolescence (Ages 12 to 18)

Introduction

|||||||||||||||||||||||||||||||||||||||||||||

WHO IS THE SUPER GRANNY?

You are! You don't look like the grandmothers in the picture books your own children used to have. You don't look like your own grandmothers or even your own mothers. And you don't act like any of these either. You're engaged in life, with more activities than you have time for, whether they're related to profession or politics or passions. You're more comfortable with rock 'n' roll than a rocking chair, and more likely to take to haute cuisine than bake cookies. You don't own an apron, but you're likely to own a computer, a PDA, a cell phone, a mountain bike, or a tennis racket, and definitely multiple pairs of blue jeans. You don't look—or for the most part, act—like anyone's grandmother.

But with all of this, you're thrilled to have those grandchildren and to enjoy this very special dimension of your full life. You remember what the humorist Sam Levenson once said: "Grandparents and grandchildren get along so well because they have a common enemy." You find that you're more patient, more involved, more interested in spending time with your grandchildren than you were with your own children at those ages. You have more time now, more money, and more perspective on what's important in life. You're not overwhelmed by juggling career and family, so you can freely enjoy this new generation in a way their busy parents cannot.

I often see parents talking on their cell phones while they are out with their children—walking in the street, pushing them on playground swings, or riding a bus—being more involved with the phone conversation than with the child. But I never see a grandmother opting for cell phone over child. No matter how busy we are, when we take time out from our careers and our other activities to be with our grandchildren, we know that this is an event, a precious interlude, one that we want to experience as fully as we can. We know how fast children grow up.

When I am alone with one of my five grandchildren, I often feel as if I am in a different world from my usual one, a world of the immediate present, a world in which every other activity fades into the background, a world in which I concentrate only on him or her and what he or she needs, a Zen world. It's as if I know what I'm supposed to do: I'm carrying on an ancient tradition of grandmothering and child care, and I'm totally at peace with the world and myself.

I have no memory of giving this same kind of concentration to my own small children on a day-to-day basis. In those days, my mind was like a mosaic in the making, its neurons scattered like loose tiles. Part of me was so often somewhere else, as I would think about what I had to do or felt I had to do—the marketing, the cooking, the laundering, the chauffeuring, the cleaning, the finding of babysitters—so I could work at one part-time or free-lance job after another.

Being a college-educated mother in suburban America back then meant feeling that you had to be the best at mothering and homemaking and wifeing—and at something else, too. Being a man in those days meant advancing in your career so that you could take good financial care of your family. Now, most of the young parents I know are busier than ever, with feelings of obligation to be professional-level mothers and fathers, while soaring to the top in their careers. There are, of course, multiple satisfactions in multiple roles, but as much as today's young parents treasure their fuller participation in both home and the wider world, their job is not easy. And that's where grandmothers come in.

My father's mother, Dora, the only grandmother I ever knew (Sarah, my mother's mother, whom I was named for, died before I was born), was always old to me, although at the time of my birth, she was younger than I am now. As far as I could tell, my grandmother was permanently glued to her couch, where she sat wrapped in a shawl on the warmest day. She was a sweet old lady who was always happy to see me, who smiled at me, and who told me stories about her life in the Old Country. I know that she must have left that couch from time to time during my childhood, but I have no memory of her being anywhere else until she came to my wedding and then my college graduation. I don't see her in my mind's eye as doing anything. She didn't cook, she didn't knit, she didn't play cards, and she certainly didn't play with me. As far as I know, she didn't have friends and didn't go out for fun. The only times I ever saw her were when my parents took me there or reminded me to walk a couple of blocks to go visit her. It wasn't until after Dora died that I learned of the poetry she had written over the years and of the account of her journey to the New World. She never shared these aspects of herself with me.

My friends and I inhabit a different world. Most of us don't even own a shawl—or if we do, it's a chic pashmina that we'll wear around our shoulders over a strapless dress—even sometimes when strapless is wildly inappropriate for someone of our chronological age. (As I always say, everyone has to grow old, but you can stay immature forever.) We are more likely to drive, bike, train, or fly to visit our grandchildren—even when it means taking time out from our job or other commitments—than they are to come to us. We are more mobile. And when we are with these incomparable creatures, we entertain them—and entertain ourselves—in countless ways. Yes, we tell them stories about our earlier lives, but we do so much more. We live life to the utmost, we pursue our passions, and we bring them to our grandchildren. We share ourselves and are rewarded by their interest in us. And we're spontaneous: We may plan one thing, but then discover another possibility, and can turn on a dime when we see new horizons beckoning for ourselves and our grandchildren.

Our mobile society means that we're less likely to live around the corner from our grandchildren, as my grandmother did with me. Two of my grandchildren are a two-hour drive away from my home on Long Island; the others are an eight-hour plane ride and a one-hour drive away in Europe. These days, grandmothering across the miles is often the norm. Still, we find ways.

Another change in society involves grandchildren who are very close to their grandmothers, because the grandmothers are raising them, for one reason or another. This nationwide trend, in rural areas as well as urban ones, has been increasing since the early 1990s, according to the United States Census Bureau. A number of organizations and websites have sprung up to help grandparents raising grandchildren, and virtually all of the activities in this book can be enjoyed by those of you involved in child-rearing all over again.

In the following pages, you'll read about some of the activities that we twenty-first-century grandmothers and our grandchildren have enjoyed the most. The ideas and the activities in this book come from grannies all over the United States and from other countries such as Germany, New Zealand, Australia, and India. These grannies told me their stories about what they do, or did, with their grandchildren, or in some cases, the grandchildren told me what they have done with their grannies. I hope that all these true stories about real people will inspire, inform, amuse, and fuel you with lots of good ideas for making memorable every moment spent with your grandkids. (Well, nearly every moment—let's be realistic here!) For more ideas, you can go to the Resources appendix on page 203 for helpful websites.

I'm always eager to hear about more fun activities, so if you would like to share your own great grandmothering ideas, please write to me c/o Sterling Publishing Co., Inc., 387 Park Avenue South, New York, NY 10016-8810.

Hoping to hear from you!

Sally Wendkos Olds

Sally (also known as "Oma")

How to Use This Book

Although activities in this book are grouped by age (four age groups, infancy through adolescence), you'll find that many of them fit into more than one age category, and a savvy granny can often tweak the activity to appeal to grandchildren of varying ages. The same is true of expense: Depending on how many supplies you want to buy, and where you want to buy them, or how elaborate a trip you plan with your grandchild, the cost of an activity can range from very few bucks to more than your own kids are willing to spend!

To help you choose activities, each one is matched with a series of icons (little pictures) that will give you a quick snapshot of the activity. The icons will tell you:

- the amount of cash you'll be shelling out (from free or dirt-cheap/$ to doable/$$ to only-a-granny-would-pay-for-this/$$$)
- the kind of creative activity involved (arts & crafts, music, literature)
- the level of energy required (those requiring fairly high energy, like slaloming down a mountainside, are identified with a "high energy" icon)
- activities especially suitable for long-distance super grannies (great stuff you can do to stay connected with your grandkids despite the miles—and even continents—between you)

$
free or
dirt-cheap

$$
doable

$$$
only-a-granny-
would-pay-for-this

arts & crafts

literature

music

high energy

long distance

Infancy to Age Three

You're holding your infant grandchild in your arms, and you know that life can't get any better than this. And then you feel something warm that's not the baby, and you realize that this precious being's diaper has slipped its moorings. But somehow you don't even mind. This is bliss! This is being a grandmother!

I remember a time more than twenty years ago, with my first grandchild. My schedule was busy, with looming writing deadlines, but my husband and I had carved out a week to visit our daughter and her family a couple of thousand miles away. One day during that visit, I was holding two-year-old Stefan on my lap, inhaling his sweet well-cared-for-baby fragrance, burying my face in his soft, fine hair, feeling the soft, smooth creaminess of his skin. I was not thinking about anything else, about what I should or could be doing. I was completely in and of the moment, loving it, cherishing it, just for what it was. This was a peak experience for me.

Whether you rarely see those little joys in your life, or you're lucky enough to live around the corner from your grandbabies, you can begin forging your bonds with them and *enjoying them as soon as they enter the world. And as you'll see in the following pages, sometimes we can show our love for them even before they're born! Once they're here, we grannies find myriad ways to enjoy our young grandchildren, sometimes with the help of modern technology, and at other times just by caring enough to make the time for them. You're in for a treat!*

A Quilting Community

When her daughter, Teena, told Philo that she was pregnant, Philo got busy. She contacted friends and relatives in her Newark, California, community, mostly of South Indian background, who are close to Teena, as well as Teena's close friends and cousin, and asked everyone to prepare a square for a baby quilt. The instructions were simple: Appliqué an animal shape onto a square piece of cotton fabric. Philo, an experienced needlewoman who, however, had never quilted before, would stitch the squares together and finish the quilt. Although Philo planned to surprise Teena with the quilt at her baby shower, the baby, Saheli Adiya, provided the surprise, by coming early before the quilt was ready. Neither mother nor baby minded, and the almost-finished quilt was a big hit at Saheli's welcome party.

My friend Elly, the mother of Teena's husband, Dan, chose a penguin for her square, since she had seen a penguin colony with the young couple, both physicians, when she visited them in Africa, where they were working in community health projects. Teena went to California to have her baby, and when Elly visited from her home in New York, she and Philo sewed together, and agreed that both would use orange thread to show their linkage with each other. This was one way of bringing together Saheli's Indian Catholic background from her mother's side and the American Jewish heritage of her father's family.

Both grandmothers respected each other's cultural traditions, like the adjustable gold waistband that Saheli received at 28 days of age, in the Indian belief that gold has special properties that are good for the body, and the cutting off of a lock of her hair at one month, to be saved for her, a Jewish custom. An additional cross-cultural touch in the quilt is the penguin's stomach, made from the yarmulke that Dan's father wore at a family wedding. Saheli now has a precious gift that not only supplies warmth and beauty, but will also help her learn about animals, and about her Granny (Elly) and her Ammamma (Philo) and the rest of her unique family. (Ammamma is the word for grandmother [mother's mother] in India.)

MAKING THE QUILT

Philo set the quilt's theme as *Outdoor Animals*, in recognition of Teena and Dan's enjoyment of the outdoors and the animal parks the families had visited in Africa. To make the project as easy as possible for participants with varying degrees of sewing skills ("I know my friends!" she says), she prepared extensively before enlisting help.

First, with the aid of a friend who had made quilts before and shared her special tools, Philo drew up a checklist of all that she would need to do and buy, as well as a timeline for the project. She calculated the size of the quilt she wanted and came up with one that would require twenty squares. Philo bought the cloth at a fabric store, along with pre-quilted lining, which she was lucky enough to find on a 50 percent off sale. Then she collected easy-to-sew animal patterns (like giraffe, lion, and monkey) and traced them onto transfer paper. Philo and her other daughter, Maria, transferred the animal patterns onto calico scraps and then ironed the patterns onto 6-inch off-white squares, which they gave or mailed out.

Philo told everyone that she wanted to have the quilt ready for Teena's arrival, six weeks ahead, and gave all the stitchers a deadline of three weeks. "I didn't want to give them too much time," she says, "because it's too easy to put it off and forget about it! But you need to allow yourself enough time so that you can enjoy the project and not get rushed and cranky." Philo did enjoy the project and was delighted to learn that Teena and Dan had planned an animal theme for the nursery and had ordered an animal-themed quilt, which they canceled as soon as they laid eyes on the very special cover made by many loving hands.

If she were doing it again, Philo says, she would probably organize a quilting bee at her house so that everyone could work together and enjoy the communal spirit. Grannies without a quilting expert as a friend can find help from the Internet. Type "quilting help" into your search engine and you will find thousands of helpful entries. One clear set of directions is at www.lucyfazely.com/howto/piecetop.htm.

Make Your Own
Personalized Birth Book

While Susan, an author, was sitting for many long hours in the hospital waiting for the birth of her first grandchild, she did what writers do—she wrote. She ended up with a very special book she titled *On the Day You Were Born*.

The book was so successful that she went on to produce one for each of her six grandchildren. Susan jotted down what other family members in the waiting room said, what the doctors said, what everyone did, even what they ate. After family members brainstormed possible names for the baby (sex still unknown), she added the list of names to the book. "These names, some of which are pretty silly, always make the grandchildren laugh," Susan says. Four-year-old Olivia Rose giggles to think that she might have been Oleander Rumpelstiltskin!

The books include photos of the baby, the parents, and other family members; cartoons and drawings; the weather on that day; newspaper headlines; sunrise/sunset times; what happened and what famous people were born on that day in history; and other newsworthy facts. She saves a copy of the newspaper published on that day. Susan presents each book to each child on his or her first birthday.

"The best part for me," says Susan, "is that every year I get to read each book to each birthday child, and the child gets a new sense of how special he or she is—especially to me." Over the years, the children leaf through the books and particularly enjoy the pictures. You don't have to be a professional writer or artist to produce your own personalized book for a grandchild.

MAKING THE BOOK

Begin thinking about this project even before your grandchild is born. The possibilities are limited only by your own interests and imagination.

- Well before the baby's due date (since many babies are too impatient to wait for that date to make their arrival), get a notebook that you can tuck in your purse.
- Get some folders into which you can put your notes, photos, art, and anything else that will go into the book.

  If you're lucky enough to be at the hospital on The Day, record all the events of that day, such as the time the mother went into the hospital and the time of the actual birth; the names of family members who were present; the names of the doctor, midwife, nurse, and other helpful personnel; quotes from some or all of these people; and even what people ate while waiting for the big event.
- If you cannot be present, you can still get some information, like the timetable; the baby's weight, length, hair color, etc.; names of medical personnel; what you were doing that day (maybe taking care of an older sibling), and so forth.
- If your grandchild was adopted, adapt the book to tell his or her story in as much detail as you can.
- Write up a brief entry about what the day was like for you, and as much as you can, for what it was like for the baby,

the parents, and any siblings. Susan has written some entries from the point of view of an older sibling.

- Take or obtain photos of the baby from birth through the first year; of family members, like aunts, uncles, and cousins; of the family pet; of the family's home; and of the medical people, the hospital, and anything else you want.

- Use art too. Cut out pictures from magazines, use clip art from your word processing program, or go to a website. (Google "Coloring Pages Doctor," for example.) One site, **www.preschoolcoloringbook.com/color/cpdoc.shtml,** gives line drawings of doctors, which you can print out and adapt to suit (adding a mustache or changing a hairdo to resemble the baby's obstetrician).

- Paste photos or art on the page, or insert them using your computer program (and scanner, if necessary). Make color copies of any pages with visuals so that they will be easier for the child to handle.

- To get information on this day in history, go to a website like **www.scopesys.com/anyday, www.infoplease.com/dayin history,** or **http://memory.loc.gov/ammem/today/today.html** (this one has illustrations you can insert in your book).

- For the book itself, use an inexpensive fake-leather-bound album, a three-ring notebook, or any other style. Once you have assembled your entries, you'll know how big an album or notebook you'll need. Use stick-on gold letters on the cover for the book title and the child's name.

Your unique first-birthday present is now ready, to be cherished for a lifetime!

Write Love Letters

One month after Alison, Joan's first grandchild, was born seventeen years ago, Joan sat down and wrote her a letter to welcome her to the family. Since then, Joan has written monthly letters to Alison and to her seven other grandchildren, now ranging in age from seven to seventeen. The children live in New Jersey, Ohio, and Kentucky, many miles away from Joan's home in Largo, Florida, and the correspondence is a brilliant way for Joan to be a vibrant presence in their lives. She handwrites all the letters, and in each one she reminds the grandchild about his or her age in months. So far, she has written more than 1,200 pieces of mail and she says, "I will continue to do so until I am no longer on this earth."

How did this epistolary relationship start? "My mother was an avid letter writer, but after she died, I realized that I didn't have a sample of her handwriting, and I always felt bad about that." Joan decided that her grandchildren would not have to wonder what her "scribble" looked like.

Joan's notes—true love letters—start out, "Happy first (or whatever) birthday." They then go on from there, and as the number of grandchildren increased to eight, Joan did the same for each one, and still does. Every month of their lives, on the day when they were born, they have received a handwritten note or letter from Grammy (or Gramma, depending on the grandchild). Joan usually writes about their activities and how proud she is of their accomplishments, which include playing a musical instrument, taking Irish dancing lessons, entering competitions, and such other pursuits as soccer, golf, scouting, and church activities. Each letter is written personally to that child.

SIT RIGHT DOWN AND WRITE A CHILD A LETTER

Even in these days of email and text messages, children love to get real mail. I still get excited myself when I open the mailbox and find a handwritten envelope with my name on it. And for children, who don't receive much mail (not even junk mail), there is something special about knowing that someone took the time to compose a few words meant for you alone, and then put on a stamp, addressed and licked the envelope, and got it to a mailbox.

Joan urges grandmothers to celebrate the birth of first, and subsequent, grandchildren by getting out pen and paper and welcoming them to the world. It's often hard to relate to grandchildren on a one-to-one basis, especially when, as is so often the case these days, they live far away and your visits with them may be rushed and hectic. In a letter, you can be as personal as you want, without having to worry about interruptions from a sibling, a ringing cell phone, or some other distraction. And a major plus is that you sometimes receive a loving reply. (It's good to remember the day of the month of your grandchildren's birthdays: One set of grandparents won the Mega Millions jackpot by putting in the birthdays of their six grandchildren!)

Although I'm light years away from being in Joan's league, I do write to all my grandchildren from time to time, but less frequently now that four out of the five correspond by email. Yet I still write often enough to warrant making regular trips to the post office, where I buy colorful commemorative postage stamps that I think they'll enjoy. I also use special stationery. My most recent missive was on a sheet of paper that had a picture of a horse that Nina and I found on the Internet and that she crayoned a bright purple. What other color would you make a horse?

And Linda, a New Zealand grandmother who writes regularly to her grandchildren in Hong Kong and Australia, says, "It's quite hard keeping up a one-sided correspondence when the children are tiny, but it establishes connections you can build on."

Sing, Sing, Sing!

When three-year-old Heather phones her grand-mother, Lana, by pushing the speed-dial key on her home phone, she says, "Gamma, we sing now!" Lana, a professional flutist, has a beautiful voice, and she has used her extensive musical training with her two grandchildren from the time they were only a couple of months old.

Lana has taught the babies *solveggio,* a worldwide system of using syllables (like "do, re, mi") to sing music that the singer has never known before, and also the hand signals in the Dalcroze system, both of which teach communication skills long before a child becomes verbal. (In the movie *Close Encounters of the Third Kind,* the military people, wondering how they would be able to speak to the aliens who had come to Earth, solved the problem with the Dalcroze eurythmics books.)

"Aside from the fun we have together," Lana says, "the singing we do develops the children's hearing and comprehension skills, and both the singing and the hand gestures teach them to communicate on a whole different level."

Now Heather will say the one word *boat,* which tells Lana that she wants to sing "Row, Row, Row Your Boat," one of the thirty or so songs in her repertoire. Some of Heather's other favorites are "Frère Jacques," "Camptown Races" (especially the "doo-da" parts), "My Bonny Lies Over the Ocean," and "He's Got the Whole World in His Hands."

BRINGING MUSIC INTO A GRANDBABY'S LIFE

You don't need to have musical talent! When I graduated from high school, our chorus teacher gently singled out one other student and me for special attention. "Girls," she said quietly to the two of us just before commencement, "you can move your mouths if you want to, but please don't sing." When my children were young and our family used to go for long car rides, I would belt out "Working on the Railroad," "She'll Be Comin' Round the Mountain," "This Little Light of Mine," and all the other lively songs I knew. The girls would exchange knowing looks until inevitably someone was bound to say, "Mo-o-om! It's okay if you don't sing." And then my grandchildren were born.

The first time I cared for my granddaughter Anna at bedtime posed a challenge, since she had always gone to sleep nursing in her mother's arms. It had been many years since I had breastfed my babies, and despite all that I had read about grandmothers in some indigenous societies being able to produce milk after decades away from Mammary Lane, I was not about to test the proposition. And so I cradled the chubby towhead in my arms, opened my mouth, and crooned (probably out of tune). After I went through the two lullabies I knew, I segued to the torch songs whose words and whose (approximate) tunes I had learned by heart in my lovesick high school days. And so a tradition began, and Anna gradually fell asleep listening to "Paper Doll," "Be Sure It's True When You Say I Love You," "Dancing in the Dark," and other relics of my old favorite radio station. Grandchildren are the best audience ever!

You can also sing your favorite songs onto a cassette or a CD, and send them with a request to the baby's parents to play them while showing a photo of you. To find the words to songs you used to know, buy a book of songs with lyrics, or go to a website like one of these:

- For kids' songs: **www.BusSongs.com** or **www.kididdles. com/lyrics**
- For folksongs: **www.mudcat.org** (this one also gives instructions for making your own musical instruments)
- For popular (or once-popular) love songs: **www.romantic lyrics.com**

Stay Close Half a World Away

When New Zealander Susan's daughter married an American, she knew that she would not be able to see the young couple as often as she would like. But they stayed in close touch by phone, email, and visits once or twice a year. When her grandson Henry was born, though, the 19-hour time difference and the 10,000-mile (16,100-kilometer) distance between Auckland and Chicago yawned much too great. One way Susan bridged the gap was to set up an account by which she could talk free or for very low rates, and, with the installation of a webcam (a camera attached to her daughter's computer for online communication), she could also see Henry in real time. Susan could see him smiling, sitting up, and eventually running around the room throwing a Frisbee, imitating his father, an Ultimate Frisbee player.

Susan also set up a webcam on her own computer so that Henry (and now his little sister, Molly) can see her and become familiar with her face and her voice, so that when they do see each other, they will know that she is Susan. She had asked that the grandchildren call her "Susan" because, as she explains, "I thought that they would occasionally hear talk of me in other contexts and that would optimize their knowledge of me."

HOW TO TALK AND SEE YOUR GRANDCHILDREN LONG-DISTANCE

Several companies provide this sort of setup. Susan and her children made their connection through Skype. "I cannot speak highly enough about Skype," Susan says. "It has had benefits that I could have never predicted, as it greatly enhances not only your relationship with your grandchildren, but also with your own child. Young parents just love showing off their kids to an admiring audience, and grandparents just love looking, so everybody is very well pleased and excited."

To use Skype, download the communications software from **www.skype.com.** For worldwide communication via computer on both ends, Skype is free. For computer-to-landline (SkypeOut), it is *very* inexpensive. Once Skype is downloaded, choose your Skype name (for example, mine is "Sallyo920") and add the other Skype names you want to communicate with. To do this, access your Skype site by clicking the "Skype" icon on your desktop: Choose "Contacts, Add."

To speak to and see your grandchildren, you need the following:

- Internet connection: The faster your connection, the better your experience.
- Microphone: Some computers come with a built-in mike, but for others you have to buy one. More expensive mikes provide a crisper, clearer sound. Leave your mike plugged in even when you're not using it.
- Headset: Not essential, but it can improve the sound quality so that you can hear each precious word. This works better too if you leave it plugged in.

- Webcam: The fun part, seeing those beautiful grandkids and letting them see you! There are a number of choices for webcams (most ranging between $35 and $85) and for free accounts to use them with. A good webcam has a movable head and tripod so that you can change the angle easily. The more money you can part with, the better the image you'll see. If you're buying a new computer, you can have the webcam built in. Some webcams have microphones built in. You can turn your webcam off for bad-hair days, so you can't be seen.
- A long cord: Lets you back up, scan the room, and show other people and/or the family dog.

Another factor to consider before deciding which free service you want to open an account on is whether or not you are both using Macintosh computers, PCs, or a combination of the two. For PC users, www.hotmail.com is one choice. For Macs, you have to use Skype or AOL.

Another company, Jajah, allows you to use your landline or cell phone to place and receive calls. Calls are free if both parties are Jajah members and usually less than a cent a minute if only one party is a member. Webcams don't work with Jajah. For information, go to www.Jajah.com.

Some helpful links:

http://en.wikipedia.org/wiki/Webcam
http://en.wikipedia.org/wiki/Skype

Play Games

When Chris's own children were little, she made up "Gotcha!" a game that she has played with all her grandchildren and currently plays with sixteen-month-old Tyler. First, Chris gently grabs Tyler's hand and says "Gotcha!" Then she lets Tyler get her hand and says, "Tyler got Grandma!" The first few times they played, Chris would say the phrase even if Tyler touched her someplace else. "Gotcha!" is Tyler's favorite game. He laughs when Chris gets his hand, but he likes it better when he gets Grandma. When he started to understand the game, he would hold out his hands and Chris would snatch hers in and out very fast so that he couldn't get her, but if he seemed frustrated, she would make it easy for him to get her. "Now," Chris says, "he actually does get me and I don't have to let him win."

When Chris told me about another game she plays with Tyler ("I make my eyes and tongue both go right and then left, or the other way, and it sounds so stupid, but it makes him laugh. He can't do this yet, although he's trying."), it brought back memories of a game my father, Sam Wendkos, used to play with my children, and that I have played with my grandchildren.

You have the child touch your nose with her finger, and when she does, you stick out your tongue. When she pulls your left ear, you move your tongue to the left; when she touches your chin, your tongue goes back into the middle of your mouth;

when she pulls your right ear, your tongue moves to the right; and finally, when she pulls at your neck (where an Adam's apple would be), your tongue disappears back into your mouth. Sure, it's silly, but they all loved it. One reason it's so popular is that this gives the child what psychologists call *agency*: By their own actions, they can make other things happen.

WHICH GAMES TO PLAY

The possibilities for games to play with babies are limited only by your imagination and your willingness to look and act ridiculous! Fran puts a napkin in her mouth and shakes her head wildly, which makes her grandbaby laugh like crazy. Grandmothers who don't worry about looking silly have the most fun.

Then there are the old standbys like "This Little Piggy," in which you touch each toe and say or sing the nursery song, "This little piggy went to market," etc. Or you imitate the baby's actions (opening his mouth wide or moving his head around). Chances are that the baby will do it again to keep the game going. You will get tired before he does.

Chris, who plays many games with all three of her grandchildren, makes a key point: "I think it's important to watch the child's responses and adapt to them. Sometimes something that most children like won't work at all with one child, so you drop it and go on to something else."

For more ideas for baby games, buy the little card set "52 Activities for You and Your Baby" by Lynn Gordon (Chronicle Books, 2003).

Talk with Your Hands

*T*wo-year-old Nicholas was asleep when his grandmother, Sandy, arrived. As soon as he saw her, he ran over to her and said, "Happy Birthday, Bam!" Then he pointed to his eye, then pointed to his heart, then pointed to Sandy, and then put both hands up like goal posts, palms outward, fingers spread apart. Translation: "I (eye) LOVE (heart) YOU (Sandy) DEARLY (hands up)." Perfect gestural language!

Babies learn gestures long before they learn how to speak. By about nine months, they begin to use gestures to communicate, coming up with some on their own, like holding up their hands to show they want to be picked up and pointing to something they want. They learn to wave bye-bye, nod their heads to say yes, and shake their heads to signify no. By about a year, they use more elaborate gestures, like holding an empty cup to their mouth to show they want a drink. And they can be taught many more, including the formal ones that are part of American Sign Language (ASL) through which people with hearing disabilities communicate.

It's great fun to make a game out of teaching gestures to babies and toddlers, as Sandy did. Even one-year-olds can learn to blow to mean "hot," to sniff to mean "flower," and so forth. And you'll be rewarded by easier—and sometimes amusing—

communication, as Sandy was when she took Nicholas to a small ranch and handed him a warm, just-laid egg. Nicholas tried to chase down the chicken to give her back her egg, but when Sandy explained that it was a gift from the chicken, Nicholas said "thank you" to the chicken in sign language.

TEACH YOUR GRANDCHILD TO SIGN

You may be able to find workshops or classes in teaching babies to sign at your local "Y" or other community organization. Also, there is plenty of help on the Internet. One very helpful website is **www.signingbaby.com,** which breaks down information into categories ("Why sign?", "Advantages," "What's Involved," "Get Started," "Helpful Hints," etc.); shows photos and videos of babies signing; sells books, CDs, DVDs, and flash cards; refers you to research; and provides links to classes and workshops.

A major plus to teaching babies to sign (besides the fact that you'll both have a good time!) is that it can help take the mystery out of what your grandchild wants—or doesn't want—which brings you a step closer to helping him or her be happier.

When your grandchild is about six months old, choose one sign to start with. "Need-based" signs include those for milk, eat, drink, change (diaper), hot or cold, and bed/sleep. Or pick a sign about something the baby is already excited by, like Mommy, Daddy, the family dog, or something else that she or he likes to watch, like a ceiling fan. Say, you pick the sign for milk: Open and close your fist as if you were milking a cow, make this sign every time you give milk to the baby, and say the word *milk* at the same time. When your grandbaby begins to sign back to you, choose another sign and work on that, while still reinforcing the first sign.

The keys to success include consistency (making the sign every time), variety (doing it in different settings), praise, your obvious enjoyment, and patience. You'll learn the signs along with your grandbaby, and in no time at all, you'll both have an extensive vocabulary.

Art Appreciation Pre-101

Almost from birth, two-year-old Makaela has been spending two days a week, with one overnight, with her grandparents in Marin County, California, and it's hard to say who enjoys the time more. One interest Makaela already shares with them is art. Richard and Terry's walls are vibrant with colorful paintings, which they talk to Makaela about. When Makaela was about ten months old and barely crawling, she would thrust out an arm and point to some painting on the wall, making it clear that she wanted to see it from a closer perspective. So Grandma Terry would hold her up to the work and tell her something about it, sometimes describing the colors. Richard or Terry might talk about the subject of the painting and something about the artist, like "This is a picture of flowers painted by my cousin, Dorri, or this is a fair painted by your great-grandmother," even knowing that Makaela had never seen a fair and couldn't know what a Ferris wheel is. Or they might point to the cats in a batik hanging and count them, or the flowers, or the birds around the cats.

From the beginning, Makaela's grandparents have generally talked to her as if she is much older and understands everything they say. And the more they do this, the more she understands. After her grandparents say something, Makaela may say "more," meaning she wants to hear it again. Since both Terry and Richard are retired, they glory in having the time to be patient.

If Makaela then points to another painting, they go to that one, and so on, until she seems satisfied. She appears more interested in some paintings than in others. Is the toddler a budding art critic? Or do her preferences for the paintings in her room and the family room reflect the fact that these are the rooms she spends the most time in? Does it matter?

Makaela also enjoys watching two items that swing from the ceiling: a sleek mobile and a stuffed toucan. When Terry discovered Makaela's interest in the mobile, she would blow on the mobile to get it to rotate and hold Makaela up to see it. Makaela loved watching the movement, and it didn't take long before she would pucker her own lips to imitate blowing.

SHARING YOUR LOVE OF ART

Makaela visited her first art museum at fourteen months of age, where she wandered around, with grandparent-docents following closely behind. At twenty months, she went to an art installation where visitors could interact with the exhibits, two of which she wanted to see over and over again.

At two, she enjoys looking at *Mini Masters* board books (Round Table Press), which stay at her grandparents' home. Each book shows paintings by a famous artist, like Picasso, Cassatt, and Renoir, and a boxed set of four books shows paintings by Degas, Van Gogh, Matisse, and Monet. Simple rhyming text accompanies each painting, and the books receive five-star reviews from www.amazon.com buyers. Makaela will ask, "What's this, Grandma?" or "What's happening?" And she revisits her experiences of the day by explaining pictures to her stuffed animals: "Look at this, Bobo! Pigeons!"

Although it may sound as if her grandparents have a concerted plan to develop Makaela's interest in art, they consider Makaela's interest in art simply an extension of her interest in everything. Her trips to museums are like her visits to the park or the zoo, and the nature of the jaunts is not much different. "We just let her explore," says Terry, "and we talk to her about her surroundings."

$

Bathtub Adventures

When the very youngest of my friend Barbara's six grandchildren (all of whom are under six years old) come to visit, they crawl to the bathroom and start throwing toys in the tub. The older ones say, "Savta [the Hebrew word for grandmother], I feel like a bath." Barbara's specialty is the "Adventure Bath." Bath time becomes fun time, with a wealth of bath toys and Savta's interest. Since all of Barbara's grandchildren live not too far from her home in Jerusalem, these adventures can be regular affairs.

As soon as the babies can sit up, they delight in peeling off simple toys that stick to the side of the tub and laugh with glee when Savta puts them back up. Peel off, put back—what could be more fun? (It's on the same principle as dropping spoons from a high chair, only less back strain for the retriever!) As the children get a little older, they play more sophisticated games. One favorite involves pairs of brightly colored animal shapes. The children learn to make the sounds of lions, elephants, horses, and donkeys. Then they name the animals, and finally they find matching pairs. Moving up the age ladder, the kids sail boats and play with balls and other floating toys.

These aquatic adventures can inspire creative thinking, as when Tzur, age four, playing with dinosaur stickers, contradicted Barbara's explanation that dinosaurs all disappeared from earth at once "and we're not sure why." "But we know why," Tzur announced. "A comet hit the Earth and killed them . . . and also

all the witches. That's why there are no more witches, right Savta?" Could this be the germ for a brilliant scientific career in Tzur's future? Bath time is often a late-afternoon blessing, when children and parents alike may be tired and stressed. An adventure in the tub provides a break for everyone.

PRESCRIPTION FOR ADVENTURE

You can stock up with a wide variety of inexpensive bath toys from toy stores, supermarkets, and dollar stores. There are animal stickers, boats perfect for playing "pirate," magic balls that color the bath water, and washable bath crayons to write on tub or body. You can even get the kids clean with shampoo and soap in appealing shapes, scents, and colors.

Supplies for the adventure:

- A simple open basket to store the toys and let them dry between baths.
- A low stool so that you can sit next to the tub. Most of us grannies can agree with Barbara when she says, "Squatting has its limits!" When you're comfortable, it's easier to get a conversation going, maybe about who a child's friends are or what he wants for his birthday, or how the dinosaurs disappeared.
- Fluffy towels, with hoods for the smallest bathers.
- Fun pajamas to keep on hand because, as Barbara says, "You never can tell when a grandchild might show up for a bath!" When parents take the freshly bathed and PJ'd child home, with a good part of the bedtime ritual already taken care of, everybody's happy and appreciative of Granny's bath adventures.

Low-Tech, High Rewards

"My grandmom has taught me since I was born," says Rebecca, age fourteen. Marjorie has been able to do this even though, like many of us grannies, her home (in Bala Cynwyd, Pennsylvania) is not nearly close enough to her grandchildren (in Maryland). But she hasn't let the miles stop her from being a strong presence in her grandchildren's lives, nor has she been stopped by modern technology. "I don't do email and I don't do the Internet," she says. "I'm a Luddite."

What Marjorie does do is communicate. For example, from the time Becca, the oldest grandchild, was two years old, Marjorie has been writing to her once a week. She would often send puzzles and cartoons that she would clip from her local newspapers, and would always try to include a photo of a baby zoo animal or a sailing ship or some other picture that would appeal to a child. "I'm notorious for sending clippings," she says, "and this habit was a natural for my grandchildren.

"Even though I don't see them as often as I would like, I can still take opportunities to do things with them, and for them, that they will be able to do throughout their lives." Becca remembers how Marjorie taught her how to use a screwdriver by putting screws in a bar of soap and how she introduced her to many favorite books and still sends new ones. "We would go to the Bala Library," Becca says. "And now I have my own miniature library with all the books she's given me."

STAYING IN TOUCH–AND TEACHING TOO

Marjorie's background as an educator running college-level "Study-Abroad" programs has paid off in the interest she has taken in teaching her grandchildren, but you don't have to be a teacher to follow in her footsteps.

- When Marjorie started writing to Becca, she printed the letters on lined paper. Wendy, Becca's mother, read the notes aloud and gave Becca a special box to keep them in.
- One typical letter started out, "Guess what? I have a turtle in my bathtub!" and in one page went on to tell what he looked like, how he was found, and how she happened to house him. The letters were always conversational or topical, and always signed: "Love, x♡ x♡ , Grammom."
- When Marjorie sent photos, she included the captions. "I wanted to make reading newsprint a familiar thing so that as Becca got older, she could move on to articles."
- As Becca began to recognize words, Marjorie would underline vocabulary words and write definitions in footnotes, until Becca was big enough to look the words up herself in the children's dictionary that Marjorie had sent her.
- Later on, Marjorie started adding more extensive footnotes to her letters, thus teaching a skill that's useful now that Becca does research projects for school.

My Grandchild,
the Muse

When Rosemary's first grandchild reached his first birthday, she reached for a pen and wrote a poem in celebration. It reviewed her favorite activities with Jake over the past year—cuddling, reading to him, seeing him smack his lips over his yogurt, holding his hand as he learned to walk, and capturing his personality, as in:

> *"Your disposition is so sweet and your personality so engaging,*
> *It's no wonder that everyone smiles at you and just loves gazing."*

Rosemary found that she enjoyed writing poems, which she had never done before. They helped her savor precious memories, and she began to write them regularly. Between her visits to Jake in Chicago from her home in Los Angeles, she would send new poems, combining them on the page with pictures of Jake and herself. And when Jake's twin brothers, Evan and Zach, came along, they received their own odes, including this:

> *"We had so much fun with you while Mommy and Daddy*
> *went on vacation*
> *At the zoo, out to breakfast, and for walks to the park near*
> *the train station."*

Other verses followed, for birthdays, for special occasions, for the time Jake underwent surgery and had to spend time in a cast, for passing on values, and for communicating love:

> *"The moon is truly an awesome sight, right up there for*
> *   all to see,*
> *And it is even more special for us—Jake, Evan, Zach,*
> *   Papa and me.*
> *It reminds us all that our love for each other is grand &*
> *   always in play,*
> *Even when we are miles across the country and so very*
> *   far, far away."*

All the boys look forward to new "grandma poems" and love rereading the old ones every time Rosemary comes for a visit. And in between visits, their parents read the poems aloud, continuing Grandma's presence in the children's lives.

POEMS FOR YOUR GRANDCHILDREN

Even if you have never written a poem in your life, seeing the face of your first grandchild may inspire you to pen a few lines. You don't have to be Emily Dickinson to produce charming, creative poetry—or to be appreciated by your grandchildren. Even before they can understand the words, they can hear the lilt in your voice as you recite to them. And if you make a tape recording or video, or speak to them through a webcam, they will get to know and appreciate Grandma the Poet even more. If you get serious about your poetry, you can sign up for a poetry writing workshop in your local adult education program, a nearby university, or online. Or you can find a book about writing poetry by going to **www.bn.com**, the Barnes and Noble website, and search for "writing poetry."

Two titles are *Poetry Handbook,* by the celebrated poet Mary Anne Oliver, and *Poetry Matters: Writing a Poem from the Inside Out,* by Ralph J. Fletcher. Instead of, or in addition to, writing your own poems, have fun reading poems to your grandchildren that have been written by others. Mother Goose rhymes are always popular with babies and toddlers, and some of my own favorite books of children's poems are by John Ciardi, A. A. Milne, and Shel Silverstein. You will find a wealth of resources by typing "poetry for children" into your search engine. And you'll quickly attain the title of Poet Laureate in your own family.

Definitely Digital

As an ardent photographer, Barbara has five ideal subjects: her grandchildren, ranging in age from one to eight years old. Madeline, eight, has loved taking pictures herself since her trip three years ago to Disney World, when Madeline used Barbara's digital camera. (Barbara then bought Madeline her own inexpensive digital, but Madeline likes Grandma's better.) Madeline filled the card with photos of Mickey Mouse, Goofy, and friends, and Barbara created a slide show of the pictures, which she put on a CD. Whatever activities Barbara does with her grandchildren—whether it's the zoo, the pool, a bicycle ride, or a visit to New York City—get memorialized in pictures.

One of one-and-a-half-year-old Chloe's favorite activities is watching a slide show of herself and her cousins (all photos taken by Grandma) to the tunes of "Baby Beluga." Barbara taught herself how to make the musical slide shows, using Corel Photo Album (Version 5), and Windows XP's Real Player to download the music.

For beginning photographers, digital cameras are great; the child can click the shutter as often as she wants, and you and she can decide together which ones to delete. (When I moved up to digital, I offered to give my seven-year-old granddaughter my old film camera, and my daughter said, "Thanks, but no thanks—she'll just take zillions of pictures, and it'll cost a fortune to develop them.") Nine out of ten digital photos never do get developed.

FOR CAMERA BUGS

Once you have the digital pictures you want, you can transfer them to your computer and let your imagination run wild. You can make slide shows, collages, or books (see page 41 for Marilyn's book about Leah's journey from China). You can email them and put them on CDs, to the accompaniment of music.

Of course, not every grandmother can—or wants to—spend hundreds of dollars on a good digital camera for a young child. And not every youngster can deal with the complexities of a digital. One grandmother advises: "Get the cheapest one possible, because it is likely going to be broken, lost, or stolen pretty early on." So there is still a place for a simpler camera. The next time you take your young grandchildren to the zoo or some other photo-op spot, you can buy each of them a disposable camera and a little scrapbook. Later you can pick up your prints and together paste photos, brochures, and other mementos of the trip in the scrapbook, ending up with a souvenir of your visit.

Or you can buy one of a number of digital cameras made especially for children and selling for between $50 and $70. The reviews on these cameras are mixed, with some parents and grandparents feeling they are the perfect choice for a preschooler and others feeling they're a waste of money. If you type into your search engine "digital cameras for children," you can access sites with user reviews of the various models.

Meanwhile, you can carry a camera around with you and shoot a few photos of your day. You can ask a friend to take shots of you waving, smiling, blowing a kiss, or hamming it up some other day. Kids love it when adults aren't afraid to be wacky. Just not in front of all their friends in a classroom! You can post your photos on your blog or website, or attach them to an email message, so that when you're telling your grandchild about something you did, they'll have a fun visual to hold their interest.

$

Granny Has Fun

My friend Fran is unique, and her very special personality shows up in the sometimes wacky times she has with her grandchildren.

She is the only person I know who has invited her granddaughters to take part in a dog wedding. One June day when Avery, age five, and Zoe, age four, were visiting Meema (Fran) on Long Island from their home in London, she dug out some old veils and scraps of cloth and let the girls dress her two aging and good-natured dachshunds as bride and groom. Since the roses in Fran's garden were in bloom, the girls asked for—and got—permission to pick a few so that they could strew petals down the aisle. She's also the only grandmother I know who dresses up from time to time in a frothy gown, complete with wand and tiara, as the Tooth Fairy, or sometimes Glinda, the Good Witch. And then there are the "fairy" parties she hosts with the girls (including Charlie, who came along later), with all the little things she makes and collects: walnut shells for fairy houses, sesame seeds for fairies' dinner, and old dollhouse furniture for wee little kitchens. For years, Fran has collected tea sets wherever she could find fanciful cups and saucers that lend themselves to being used for tea parties.

When grandson Henry came along, the nature of Meema's fun shifted. Now her visits to two-and-a-half-year-old Henry in Chicago usually feature one of his favorite activities, riding in the elevator. As soon as he was big enough to reach the button on the ninth floor where he lives with his family, his favorite activity consisted of calling the elevator and then one by one pushing the buttons for every one of the fourteen floors in the apartment building, getting off at each stop, looking around, then ringing for the elevator again and getting off at the next stop. Henry's favorite outing with Meema involves going to his favorite supermarket in a large galleria with three different elevators. What bliss! "Who but a grandmother would have time to do this?" asks Fran.

PLAY TIME

"One key is listening and never being in a rush," says Fran, attributing her enjoyment of the elevator rides to her easygoing attitude. I can resonate to this. Even though so many of us contemporary grandmothers are still pursuing our own careers and have multifaceted lives ourselves, when we set aside time for the grandchildren, it's all theirs. Unlike their mothers, who are usually juggling home and work, we're not harried by our other duties. When I take my granddaughters shopping, I'm not focusing on when we get finished and how soon they need to make up their minds; I am with them for as long as they want to spend. I don't care how many pairs of jeans they try on, how many shirts they pull over their heads, how many pairs of shoes they slip their feet into. This is time I have set aside just to be with them.

But Fran's fun times with her grandchildren—including now one-year-old Molly—also owe their success to her creativity, her originality, and to wanting to play. Fran's prime play space is her kitchen. As a professional caterer, food is her palette, and so cooking and serving and eating ("Everybody likes to eat," she says) often take center stage in play as well as in work, and if a mess results, well, so what? "Kids love to play in flour, and most moms aren't so ready to let them do this. Me—I don't care."

Fran's grandchildren seem to know that no matter how old Meema gets, she will always have that sense of child's play.

Create and Publish
Your Own Book

Three-year-old Leah's very favorite going-to-bed book, which she asks her mother to read to her over and over—and over—again, is by her favorite author, her grandmother (and my friend, Marilyn). The colorful book, *The Story of Leah's Amazing Journey from Nanning, China, to America,* is by Granny Mazzy.

The 45-page book with photos and text on every page tells the story of the first year of Leah's life. It begins with her early months with a foster family in China, goes on to her mother and grandmother's trip to the Chinese placement agency in Nanning to meet Leah and take her back to Atlanta, where she now lives with her mother, Susan, and concludes with her welcome party, showing Leah sitting on an enormous stuffed lion.

Marilyn created the entire book on her computer. She scanned and downloaded photos of Leah and the important people and places of her early life, wrote the text, chose the layout, and ended up with a professional-looking keepsake, with copies for Leah herself and for other family members. "When Leah asks, 'How did I get here?' all we have to do is show her the book," says Marilyn. "It's much easier than the birds-and-bees talk."

CREATING THE BOOK

"It took a long time for me to do this, I made mistakes along the way, and I got very frustrated," Marilyn says. "After all, it involves learning a new computer program, which is no day at the beach. But then again it's only because of computers that you can do this kind of thing. And when I see how much Leah loves it, it was worth every minute."

Other grandmothers have made similar books around family reunions, trips with a grandchild, and the birth of a baby. Marilyn created her book using the online service **www.shutterfly.com**. (To find and compare different companies, type "create photo book" into your search engine and you'll find many services to choose from.)

The basic process is similar for various sites. First you join (membership is free), and then you choose from a wide array of book sizes, styles, and formats. At this writing, the 8" x 8" hard-cover book that Marilyn made costs $29.95 for the first 20 pages and $1 for each page after that (plus shipping), to a maximum of 100 pages. You can display 30 to 100 photos over 20 pages. The Shutterfly site offers a demo, which gives an overview of the process, and once you begin, it provides step-by-step directions. And to make your job easier, you can telephone for technical support at every stage of creation.

Apply Insights from Your Travels

oday's grandmothers are more likely than ever to travel, and often to exotic places where we learn new ways of looking at life.

A few days after I came home from my first visit to Badel, a remote hill village in the Himalayan kingdom of Nepal where I stayed with local families, my husband, Mark, my youngest daughter, Dorri, and I were celebrating Mother's Day at the home of my eldest daughter, Nancy. While Nancy and her husband went out for a walk, Mark, Dorri, and I stayed at their house with ten-month-old Anna. In the warm sunlight of this balmy afternoon, there we were: Mark was doing some sort of spring work in the yard, Dorri was catching up on lost sleep on the deck, and Anna and I were sitting on a bed sheet spread out on new grass under the shade of an old magnolia tree.

I started to get up to fetch one of the innumerable primary-color educational toys that Nancy takes such joy in buying for her little daughter. And then I remembered all those wonderful bright-eyed babies in Badel, and it suddenly hit me. No, Anna doesn't need any *thing* to play with. And indeed she didn't. She had me, she had the lawn, she had her own new motor skills to occupy and enchant her—she had a world of delights. She had no need to be entertained by anything called a toy. Instead, she kept herself busy pulling up shoots of grass, climbing onto my lap, reaching for my shiny earrings, moving from one position to another, pointing to birds overhead, feeling the breeze in her hair, taking in the big beautiful outdoors. So this very basic elemental sensual experience of the natural world remains always new, with a new appreciation on my part gleaned from my glimpses into another culture.

BRING YOUR TRAVELS HOME

When my friend and trekking buddy Marge came back from her first trip to Nepal, she presented a slide show to the kindergarten class that her granddaughter Martha was in, and she talked to the children about Nepal. Now Martha is in college and she remembers how proud she was of her grandma! Marge kept her talk short and showed mainly pictures of the Nepalese children, since children like to hear about children in other countries and see pictures of their houses and schools, which in this case were very different from those in the Chicago suburb where Martha was going to school.

This is a good way to show children how what we take for granted in our culture is experienced so differently in other lands—like putting diapers and pants on babies. My older grandchildren enjoyed hearing about my efforts when I was in China to find a pair of overalls for my youngest grandchild, then a toddler, which were stymied when I couldn't find a pair that weren't split down the middle to make it easier for the child to eliminate. (The parents learn very early when they need to hold the baby away from them, and the children learn early when they need to take care of business.) When I tell these stories to my grandchildren, it widens their horizons too, and after an initial, "Why do they do it that way?" (implicitly asking, "Why don't they do it our way?"), they understand that although there are many universals among people around the world, every culture has its own distinct ways of doing so many different things, that our way of thinking is not the only way.

The Preschool Years (Ages Three to Six)

"Play wit me, Nana," Connie's granddaughter begs. Our grandchildren now make giant leaps beyond the toddler stage. They speak better and understand more, they build and retain memories, they enjoy transports of imagination, and they can do more with their arms, their legs, and their little fingers. With all their changes, our opportunities to interact with them in more and more ways grow astronomically. These are the years when "playing pretend" and dressing up can spark flights of fancy, when stories and pictures in books come to rousing life, when silly word games give rise to gales of giggles, when messing about in flour and cookie dough can inspire a budding cook. The urge to create becomes paramount, whether that spark is reflected in drawing and painting (on paper or walls), building houses (from blocks or gingerbread), or making music (singing or plinking on piano keys).

These are also, of course, years when new bursts of energy and new abilities make running, skipping, jumping, and hopping fun, and when we rediscover how much fun they are for us when we're doing them with the grandkids. Getting *down and dirty in a mud puddle is something you haven't done for a while!*

Because they can remember us better between visits, our visits mean more to them. And as you'll see in this section, the pursuits we follow with our grandchildren become more varied and more complex as we enjoy different kinds of activities and stay in touch between one activity and another.

$ $

Engage Your Grandchild with the World Wide Web

Wendy, a grandmother of six, ranging in age from infancy to age six, is lucky enough to live near all her grandchildren in Melbourne, Australia. She also considers herself lucky to be able to take care of the children often, one at a time, for an afternoon or a day, to spend this special one-on-one time. When deciding what to do with each child, Wendy takes into account the child's age and interests. Wendy used four-year-old Lachlan's interest in dinosaurs to work with the computer. She sat Lachlan down in front of her computer, and together they searched for information and pictures of dinosaurs. When they found good, simple pictures that Lachlan liked, she printed out a few, gave him a box of crayons, and let him color to his heart's content. She hung one of the pictures in her house and gave him the rest to take home.

SEARCH THE INTERNET

From a very early age, children can be encouraged to find more information and activities through the resources of the World Wide Web. If you don't have a computer yourself, this is the time to call a relative or friend and give them the great pleasure of hosting you and your grandchild for an hour or so. Or you can find a computer with Internet access at your local public library or at an Internet café that charges modest fees.

Once you're at the screen, you can use one of the popular search engines (like (www.google.com, www.ask.com, or www.yahoo.com). But—and this is a big but—before you click on any site, be sure that you have up-to-date virus and spyware protection so that you will not infect your computer. Although most such sites are safe, you never know which one may carry a virus or worm that will damage your data.

Once you're set to search, insert your topic. For example, if you put in the search term "dinosaurs" on Google, in just a few seconds you'll get a list of more than one million sites with information about dinosaurs at more levels of complexity than you could have dreamed of (unless you're a paleontologist). If you narrow the search term down to "dinosaur coloring pages," you'll get about 300,000 sites. Some sites require registration, and some require a moderate fee to access them, but many are totally free, and you will be able to print out enough pages to cover every wall in your house! Another option is to use a computer paint program to color the pictures online.

Decorate Your Bathroom

We live in an old house. The walls of our upstairs bathrooms have the kind of white ceramic tiles that were typical when our house was built, almost one hundred years ago. Until recently the major activity involving these tiles was keeping them clean. And then I went to stay with my friend Marge. When I went into her bathroom, I saw a mug full of colorful markers and dozens of messages and drawings on the tiles. Naturally, I left my own message, and went home with an idea.

The next week, I bought a dozen markers in different colors, took a blue one, and wrote a note over the sink in our guest bathroom, quoting an innkeeper in the Thar Desert in India who had once welcomed Mark and me, saying "Guests are like rain in the desert. Whenever you come, you are welcome."

The next time our grandchildren came to visit, I showed them the markers and invited them to write or draw whatever they wanted on the tiles. We now have a memorable and colorful art display that never fails to delight, with Maika's pictures of birds, Lisa's of her pet bunny rabbit, Nina's "beginner" words like *dog* and *cat* (with some of the letters written backward), Anna's love notes like "Get well, Oma. We all love you!" and Stefan's succinct, "I had a great time being here." And many hearts, stars, and sunbursts. Adult guests, also, get creative, and we enjoy their messages too. We're not the only ones to take pleasure in the exhibit. When we had to have the tiles cleaned professionally, the company's representative admired the display and, unprompted, said he would find a way to clean around the art.

ENCOURAGING BATHROOM ART

You can keep the exhibit relatively permanent if you supply your "graffiti" artists with permanent markers, which you can get at your local art supplies or crafts store or on line. They come in points of various sizes, ranging from ultra fine to broad; various shapes; and a wide range of colors, including metallic and fluorescent. Be sure to confirm that the ones you buy are safe to use in a small space and do not require masks or gloves.

If you want to be able to put up a changeable display, you can hang whiteboard and get special markers in your local crafts shop.

Create Your Own
Grandchild Library

he Dolphin Book Shop, the wonderful little store in Port Washington, where I have lived for almost forty years, specializes in children's books. The salespeople read all the books themselves and can always recommend the perfect book no matter what the child's age. I never get out of there without browsing the kids' books. That's how I found *Our Granny.*

How could I resist this book by Margaret Wild and Julie Vivas, with its illustrations of grandmothers blow-drying their blue hair, wearing skyscraper-high heels, driving a truck, playing a clarinet, marching in demonstrations, doing aerobics to make their wobbly bottoms smaller, and giving big, sloppy kisses? I couldn't. I brought *Our Granny* home, and I have read it to one grandchild after another, always at my house.

Of course, my husband and I buy our grandchildren their own books and have enjoyed watching all five of them grow into readers. And, of course, we help them pick out books at the library. But they all know that whenever they come to our house, they can snuggle up to us and read books that they know we love too. When Nina, age five, gets ready to climb into bed, she invariably brings an armful of my books and carefully arranges them in the order she wants them read. "Why don't you read one to me first?" I asked her that last time. And, having heard these stories so many times, she cheerfully began "reading" from memory: "Mabel wasn't always a tooth fairy. . . ."

BUILDING YOUR LIBRARY

Your "granny library" should include books that your grandchildren do not already have at home. So this eliminates *Goodnight Moon, Pat the Bunny,* and other classics. Look for books with a special angle, ask your local children's librarian, look for books you encounter on your travels, and check the book review section of your newspaper for new books.

These are some of our most successful books for our preschool grandchildren:

- *Los Tres Pequenos Jabalies,* by Susan Lowell and Jim Harris, which tells the story of the three little pigs (here, three little *javelinas,* a kind of wild pig) in English and Spanish, which we found in a bookstore in Arizona. After all, the children may study Spanish some day.
- *Mabel the Tooth Fairy and How She Got Her Job,* by Katie Davis, which stays funny after hundreds of readings. (A very important qualification for any book I bring into the house; I have to like it even on the umpteenth reading.)
- *My New York,* by Kathy Jakobsen, which tells a simple story about a young girl in New York City. My grandchildren like it because they have been to many of he landmarks pictured: the Museum of Natural History with its huge dinosaur, the Empire State Building, Chinatown, the Central Park Zoo, and other favorites. And I like it because the pictures are complex enough that I manage to find something new every time we look at them.

A Book Just for Your Family

lmost every day during a family trip to Costa Rica, five-year-old A.J. kept asking his grandparents and parents, "Do we have to take the airplane home? Can't we go home by boat? Or train? Can't we go any other way?" Immediately after they came home (via two airplanes), Grandma Lynne looked for a book for young children that dealt with the fear of flying. Since she couldn't find one, she made her own.

Lynne created a bunny rabbit family that mirrored A.J.'s own family (Mommy and Daddy Bunny, Older Brother, Middle Sister, and Younger Brother) and made up a story about airplane travel. She put the book together, with pictures and text, and presented it to the family. Now, two years later, it's A.J.'s favorite book, which he often takes to bed with him.

Now Lynne is working on another family book. After Lynne told Jake, A.J.'s thirteen-year-old brother, "When we go to Israel, you'll see a lot of young men who look like your dad," and Jake said, "I thought Israelis were all old men with beards," Lynne decided that a little knowledge was warranted. And when Becca, age eleven, asked, "Is it going to be any fun?" Lynne decided to put in pictures of camel rides, an undersea aquarium, and children playing. So now the bunnies will be going to Israel.

CREATING THE BOOK

"The more you talk to children," says Lynne, "the more you know what their questions and concerns are, and the more ideas you can get for your book." She sees A.J., Jake, and Becca at their home in Connecticut about once a week, and after their Costa Rica trip, she talked especially to A.J. His specific concerns about flying made it into the book: "'I don't like airplanes,' said Little Brother Bunny. 'They make me worry, make me nervous.'" A.J.'s questions ("How does it get up? What keeps it up there? How does the airplane get back onto the ground?") inspired Lynne's Internet research into the science of aeronautics, which she then explained in the book in very simple language.

To illustrate *The Bunny Family,* Lynne went to www.google.com, clicked on "Images," and specified terms like "airplanes," "pilots," and "rabbits." She downloaded images she wanted and printed them out on her color printer. She illustrated other pages with pictures from catalogs, which she either scanned or copied. The next stage involved pasting up pages with text (printed out in different fonts and sizes) and photos, and then copying the pages. Lynne inserted the completed ten double-sided pages into a colorful three-ring binder.

To make a grandchild's book even more personal, you could put in such extras as luggage tags, airplane boarding passes, postcards, ticket stubs from museums, and photographs of your family. "The first book had very little text—mostly pictures," says Lynne. "But the children are older now, and also this new topic calls for more explanations." By making your own book, you can tailor it precisely to your readers. The possibilities are just as great as your imagination and just as personal as your knowledge of your grandchild.

$

Eat Dessert First

Marty is a grandfather we grannies can learn from. This high-powered jet-setting attorney, who regularly flies around the world on behalf of his clients, comes home to relax at his country home in Massachusetts, where he often spends weekends with his seven grandchildren. Lest anyone think he is a doting grandfather, however, he has a definite set of rules for all the children. Marty's first rule is, "No one gets to start eating dinner until he or she has eaten his or her dessert. No dessert, no dinner."

The first time Marty announced this to four-year-old Rachel and her two-year-old brother, Sam, Rachel was incredulous. "What will Mommy and Daddy say?" she asked. "Will it be okay with them? Can we tell them?" Marty answered, "When you're with me, I'm the boss—I make the rules. Remember, I'm the parent of your parent." Still, the questions persisted: "What happens if we eat our dessert and we don't have room for our regular dinner?" "That will be just too bad for the regular dinner," Marty replied.

They went to a local restaurant where both children ordered ice cream, and then hamburgers, which this time they did have enough room for. And as soon as they returned to Marty's house, they called their parents, who have been supportive all along of Pop-pop's rules, which apply "only when you're with Pop-pop." Marty reluctantly relaxes the "dessert-first" rule occasionally, as when another set of grandchildren, Emma, age nine, and Lauren, age seven, sometimes say, "I'm hungry—can I have my dinner first, *please*?" Like any caring grandfather, Marty gives in and lets them have their main course first. "The rule works great," he says. "No one has ever eaten more than one dessert, and they often do eat their dinner afterward. And it gives me permission to eat dessert first too, one of the few privileges of age!"

GRANDPARENTS' PRIVILEGE

"Nana, you never say 'no' to me," David once told Norma. And Roberta told me, "My grandchildren love to come to my house because they get to stay up late, eat ice cream for breakfast, pretty much do whatever they want to do, as long as they don't tell their parents."

This way of grandparenting appeals to both kids and grandparents. The reason it works is that it's not an everyday affair. No parent can ever go through life without saying "no" more times than she or he would like to. But it's conceivable that a grandma or grandpa can do this. Furthermore, by this time, we've smartened up enough so that even when we want to encourage one behavior or discourage another, we usually know how to couch our answers so that the dreaded word *no* doesn't make its appearance.

Of course, for this kind of anything-goes-with-grandma, you should have the parents' agreement, or you may find that your opportunities to be with the grandkids become scarcer. It's a question of how you approach the parents and how much they appreciate your role in your grandchildren's lives.

Let's Dress Up!

With twenty-nine grandchildren from seven months of age to sixteen years, Margaret is always looking for "crowd control" activities to keep everybody happy. Just before Halloween, when seven grandchildren were visiting her home in Manassas, Virginia, for the day, she pulled out the little-girl dress-up outfits her granddaughters love, along with a pile of hats, wigs, and scarves. Then she gave each boy and girl a little bag and had them knock at two bedroom doors and the home office for "trick or treating." It was all very spontaneous and fun for everyone, and it inspired Margaret's next move.

A few days after Halloween, she bought a treasure trove of costumes in a range of sizes for 75 percent off at Wal-Mart and Kmart. Then, Margaret reports, "After Thanksgiving dinner, when the men were in the kitchen cleaning up and the moms were 'comatose' in the living room, not wanting to move or to hear a peep from any children, I took pictures of all the kids in costumes they had picked out earlier. The boys got into character, with a lot of running around and screaming in an effort to conquer their 'enemy' while brandishing their swords, fully protected with their armor." Since then, the getups have been pulled out for hours of imaginative play.

Some of the adults have gotten into the action too, so this summer, when fifty members of the family get together for their every-other-year reunion, Margaret plans to take enough outfits for everyone. Lots of cameras will be snapping, and many photos are bound to appear on Margaret's blog, "Musings on a Lazy Afternoon," at **http://margaret.theworths.org** and on the family's group email postings.

COSTUME CENTRAL

"Was there any squabbling over who got to wear which costume?" you ask. Well, gentle reader, there was not. Margaret forestalled conflicts in several ways. First of all, the varying sizes limited which garments each grandchild could wear. Secondly, she cannily led the grandchildren into the garage just a few at a time so that there was never a crowd scene like those familiar cartoons of shoppers at a department store sale. The children did not put on their outfits immediately. The "shopping" took place before dinner, and after each child had chosen his or her getup, Grandma, the wardrobe mistress, put a sticker on the hanger with that child's name and hung it in a different location, so it was no longer available. For the couple of instances when two children had their eyes on the same costume, Margaret conducted a win-win lottery, since even the "loser" got a chance to choose something else. And, too, there would always be another day.

The costume party's success rests on several criteria. Quality is one. At first, Margaret picked up odds and ends at the Goodwill store, but it was when she invested (at deep discount) in higher-quality regalia, complete with headpieces and shoes, that enthusiasm swelled. And her investment will help the whole family: As one daughter-in-law said, "I'm never buying another costume—I'll shop at Grandma's from now on."

Creativity is another criterion. You can also achieve remarkable effects by putting together "character" hats like berets and sunbonnets with silly glasses and wigs. Then there are the many possibilities unlimited by anything but your imagination: paper bags with holes cut out and decorations painted or pasted on to make unique vests; tiaras made of tinfoil paper and old beads; outfits made of black tights, tails, hoods, and "cat"-face makeup.

And then there's the labeling. "By calling it a 'photo shoot,'" Margaret explains, "everyone can dress up to have their pictures taken, in ten minutes they're done, and we have the record. Then if anyone wants to keep the costumes on, they can, but they don't have to."

"The most important thing," Margaret continues, "is having the sense of pretend, and not worrying about looking silly." I resonated to this, remembering the Halloween a few years ago when, after sending our children into the neighborhood trick-or-treating, my friend Fran, who lived next door, and I dressed up and knocked on a few doors ourselves. Our neighbors were a little surprised to see us, but rose to the occasion, and I would guess (and hope) that we were the only trick-or-treaters offered a glass of wine that evening.

Gone Fishing

As an outdoor travel expert and ardent environmentalist before most of us ever heard of global warming, it was only natural for Arline to instill a love of the outdoors in her two grandchildren. Besides taking them bird-watching, kayaking, and hiking, she has taught eleven-year-old Zoe and five-year-old Ben how to fish, and in the process, has turned them into conservationists too.

Arline took Zoe fishing at a nearby park for the first time when she was four years old. Since it was likely that they would catch fish so small they would have to release them back into the pond, Arline did not want to use barbed hooks, which would injure the fish, so they used barbless hooks with artificial worms. After baiting the hook, Arline showed Zoe how to cast, did it for her a couple of times, and then watched Zoe do it herself. She loved reeling in and casting out, and also giggled at how real the squiggly artificial worms looked.

When Zoe caught her small fish, Arline taught her how to take the hook out gently and—also gently—put the fish back into the water. As Zoe watched the fish swim away, she said, "Grandma Arline, it's good we didn't hurt it."

FISHING TIPS

Among the many entries about outdoor travel on Arline's website, www.funtravels.com, are suggestions for taking children fishing. To buy a child's fishing rod, go to www.zebco.com. For a successful fishing trip, Arlene recommends the following:

- The child has to be old enough to concentrate on what she is doing, probably at least four years old.
- Tell the child what to expect: You don't always catch a fish, sometimes the fish you do catch are too small and you have to throw them back, and you need to know whether the water you're fishing in is clean (so you can take the fish home to eat) or polluted.
- Check the license regulations in your state. Very often none is required for fisherfolk under 12 and over 65.
- Always wear sunglasses or safety glasses to prevent getting a hook in your eye.
- Always go with a partner.
- Take care of the earth. Clean up your own site, including messes left by previous anglers. Aside from preserving the beauty of nature, you will protect birds, which can swallow or get tangled in fishing lines and plastic from six-packs. And take your photos with an inexpensive real camera rather than the toss-away kind.

Decorate Tableware

Challenged by the words of Pablo Picasso ("Every child is an artist. The problem is how to remain an artist once we grow up."), my husband and I, along with our more talented children and grandchildren, have put our limited artistic abilities to work. Some years ago, when Mark and I were visiting our friend Sid, a grandfather of six, he served us dinner on melamine plates that had charming children's drawings molded into them. He told us how the plates were made, and the next time our family of grandparents, adult children, and grandchildren got together for our annual week at the seashore, everyone, from the youngest child to the oldest grandparent, made his or her own plate. In succeeding years, we have made plates, mugs, cereal bowls, hot plates, and snack trays, and more plates.

This has been a really easy activity, and everyone has enjoyed both the doing and the final products, which get a lot of use from their creators! We have ordered the basic kit—consisting of special colorful markers, special papers cut to the appropriate sizes, a mailing package, order form, and directions—from a company called Makit Products, Inc. Everyone draws a design, and I mail the designs to the company, which sends back the finished products. The activity is fun, the products make good souvenirs and gifts, and the cost is relatively modest. Not everyone has custom-designed dishes!

MAKING THE PLATES

Other companies offer the same kind of service, but we have used Make-A-Plate for more than five years (the company has been in business for thirty-seven years) and have always found their service to be excellent. This is how we did it:

- To order a printed catalog or see one online, go to www.makit.com or phone 800-248-9443. For information, send an email to info@makit.com.
- The classroom/group kits are $6.95, which include enough papers for 50 items—many more than we need, but this way we have extras for mistakes—and we have also been able to make more of a particular item at other times.
- As of this writing, the Make-A-Plate products cost $5.95 per plate, $7.95 per tray, $3.95 per coaster, $4.95 per bowl, $2.95 per calendar, $2.95 per mug, $3.95 per tumbler (long and slender), and $5.95 per hot plate.
- Many of the products also use photos, but we have not ordered these. Nor have we ordered other products, which don't have to be processed, but can be assembled at home.
- Almost all the molded products take up to fifteen working days inside the factory, but you can put in a rush order at non-holiday seasons.

Play Ball!

As a classmate of Marlyn's at the Philadelphia High School for Girls, I (a klutz whose gym teachers despaired of me) admired her athletic ability and cheered her on during school softball games. So I wasn't surprised to hear that she married a man to whom baseball has always been important, and that when Marlyn and Bob's children were young, the family's summer evenings almost always included playing ball in the park.

When grandsons came along, it was only natural for Marlyn to bring them into the family sport. She started throwing plastic balls to Spencer and Robert when they were toddlers, which they would return with their little plastic bats. When they got stronger and more proficient at about five or six years old, she started to pitch hardball to the boys to help them improve their batting and would play catch to help them get better at throwing and catching. For the past several years, whenever the boys would get together with her, their refrain would be, "Come on, Grandma, pitch me some balls" or "Let's play catch."

Robert, now age thirteen, has mostly traded his baseball bat for a guitar, but Spence, nine, hates to miss a single Little League game. Now Marlyn thinks that her hardball days may be numbered. As she says, "Last year Robert was throwing so hard that it hurt my hand, even with my catcher's mitt, and I think Spence will get to that point soon." Of course, there's always baseball as a spectator sport, and Marlyn, who lives in New Jersey, plans to use her season tickets for the local minor league team to take the boys to the games. Even though she may play less baseball, she'll still stay active. Besides lap swimming and water aerobics, she's traded the pitcher's mound for power-walking trails.

PLAYING CAN YIELD GREAT RESULTS FOR YOU

While Marlyn didn't start playing ball with her grandsons for her own personal reasons, grandchildren can give a big boost to your exercise program. For example, half an hour of pitching balls is great aerobic exercise. Pushing a stroller uphill for fifteen minutes provides good resistance training. And doing tricks with a twenty-pound toddler gives you the benefits of weight training.

Of course, you're most likely to enjoy the sports you do with your grandchildren when they're activities you do because they're fun, not because you expect results—from either you or the kids. So with a relaxed attitude, you can embark on any athletic activity.

Playgrounds Are for Grannies, Too

We're lucky to have a good playground a five-minute walk from our house, so from the time our grandchildren were toddlers, it was a must-go destination whenever they came to visit. As I would go down the sliding board and up on the swings, I have to confess that I enjoyed it as much as the grandchildren did. I must say that I'm much more sensitive to a wistful look from a child who wants to go on whatever I'm using, and, of course, I cede it right away without sulking!

These outings bring back nostalgic memories of the times I used to take my own children to playgrounds, and of the many friends I first met there, some of whom, also grandmothers by now, I still count as close friends. These days, though, I'm more interested in cultivating grandchildren's friendships. So it was a happy day a couple of years ago, when Nina was five, and was chatted up by Stephanie, a friendly redhead about her age, as they swung on adjacent swings.

Stephanie's mother noticed the camaraderie between the girls and, as she and I talked on the sidelines, invited Nina to come to her house the next day to play. She did, the girls got along famously, and now Nina has a friend in our neighborhood, two hours away from her home, and enjoys her widened social circle.

MAKING THE MOST OF PLAYGROUND VISITS

First, of course, you need to be sure your grandchild is safe. Scout out the playground ahead of time to check its safety quotient. You don't want to get there and have to leave right away with a disappointed child!

Give your business only to playgrounds with soft surfaces (like wood chips, mulch, pea gravel, rubber mats, or tiles), not hard ones (concrete, asphalt, blacktop, packed dirt, grass, or rocks). Check that all equipment is anchored safely, all pieces are in good working order, S-hooks are entirely closed, and no bolts protrude. Once there, keep close watch at all times. You want to be sure the child is playing on age-appropriate equipment (the big slide a nine-year-old would be thrilled to ride down could spell disaster for a preschooler), that there are no obstreperous children who could hurt your little angel, and that any strings on clothing are not long and loose enough to get caught on equipment.

You need to stay safe, too! I just heard about one 66-year-old woman who broke her ankle going down a slide with her two-year-old grandson. So get in shape, work on flexibility and balance, and although you don't need to act your age, you do need to remember that you may not be able to go chasing a little one on a jungle gym!

You're now free to have fun. Relive your own childhood by going high on the swings, and in the process, teach your grandchild how to pump his or her legs to keep up with you. Don't be afraid to look silly; your grandchild will think you're a great playmate. And if any budding friendships seem to be developing, don't be shy about speaking to the other child's caregiver: Most people are likely to welcome a new friend.

Create a Magical Closet

lthough Judy, known to her six grandchildren as "Gam," lives in a small apartment in Philadelphia, she enjoys the luxury of a large closet. The grandchildren enjoy it, too. Because Judy does not like to throw out anything that might someday tickle a child's fancy, over the years she has created "Gam's Magical Closet."

"My grandchildren love to come over and rummage in my closet; it is in that magical closet that their dreams are realized," Judy says. "If they need a costume for a school play, they find all the makings. We have assembled 'kings' and 'cats,' 'beauty queens,' and 'bandits.'" Posters, paints, crayons, wool, and beads lie in wait for a grandchild to make something special, and Judy is on hand to help. Even she is sometimes surprised by her discoveries: She just found butterfly masks from a long-ago trip to New Orleans nestled next to a chef's pleated white hat. "Who knows when a grandchild will be able to use these treasures?" The treasures come in handy for school projects, like the battle eight-year-old Jared depicted from toy soldiers and horses glued onto poster board.

"The key," says Judy, "is having my grandchildren come down to my level!"

COLLECTING TREASURES

Not everyone has a large closet, but most of us can make room for a chest, like the long, flat kind that fits under a bed. Judy has found many treasures (like a strip of boa feathers) from thrift shops and others (like old watches that she has made into pins) from her friends' discards. Garage sales are good sources too. One woman's trash can be another woman's (and her grandchildren's) treasure!

Judy, who made her first "magical" headband (with feathers, flowers, colored stones, and charms) for two-year-old Amy, recommends starting to collect when grandchildren are very young. "You have to do this kind of thing when the children are still interested," she said. "They grow up so fast and then have other interests."

School projects offer a wonderful opportunity for grandmas and grandchildren to interact and laugh and learn together, and to make lasting memories. You need to remember that the project belongs to the child, but grandma can make suggestions that often awaken a response in the child. If you don't want the memories to last *too* long, be careful with Krazy Glue, which, as Judy learned, can end up acting crazy, and glue your fingers together. The best glue of all is the loving relationship between grandma and grandchild!

Knit One, Purl Two

Over the past few years, the venerable art of knitting has become trendy, with fashionable men and women joining celebrities like Julia Roberts and Cameron Diaz in making scarves, caps, sweaters, and artworks that make it into museums. Martha Stewart even knitted a "liberation" scarf in jail. The most unusual item that New Haven, Connecticut, grandmother Beverly has knitted is a blue scarf for three-year-old Marisa's toy cow.

When Marisa comes to visit, Beverly introduces her to the craft she has pursued over the past thirty-five years, making hats, shawls, and socks for family and friends, and baby blankets for charity. Now she delights in Marisa's pre-knitting activities and looks forward to the day when she can teach her the finer points of the craft, as Beverly did with both her daughters. Marisa has her own tangled ball of yarn (blue, her favorite color) that stays on her bookshelf at Grandma's house, and when she wants to knit, she asks for her own needles by saying "knitting" and making knitting motions with her hands. Beverly's rule is that "knitting is sitting," either on Grandma's lap or on the living-room couch.

Marisa also loves to play with Beverly's basket of yarn. She knows she isn't allowed to take apart the skeins, and busies herself sorting them by color, learning her colors at the same time. Knitting with Marisa is unlike any other knitting Beverly has done over the years! "While I was finger-knitting the cow scarf," she says with a laugh, "Marisa 'helped' by poking her own knitting needles in and out of the yarn at the other end." Well, she was getting the idea!

GETTING STARTED

You have to know your grandchild before you start him or her off with knitting needles. A child who cannot sit still but is apt to run around brandishing the needles like swords is not a good candidate! But if your grandchild is able to sit with the needles and follow your rules, you can enjoy this activity together. It's always fun to share an activity that gives pleasure to both you and a grandchild.

Here is Beverly's advice for getting started:

- Buy either child-size knitting needles (Lion Brand or Red Heart) or two bamboo double-pointed needles (wrap small rubber bands on one end of the double-points to keep the stitches from slipping off). The best needle sizes to start with are 7s, 8s, or 9s.
- Use a smooth, light-colored, worsted-weight yarn, preferably wool or a wool blend, since wool is very forgiving. Let the child know that this is just practice yarn and that she or he will be able to select a more fun yarn (from a range that you suggest) for the first real project.
- Keep the lessons short and interesting, and be prepared to stop if the child gets frustrated or overwhelmed.
- Easy first projects might be a small doll scarf or blanket, which can be several small practice squares sewn together.

BEVERLY'S FIRST KNITTING LESSONS PLAN

LESSON ONE: Cast on two practice swatches (one for the learner and one for you to demonstrate with), and knit a base of four to six rows on each. To show how the knit stitch is formed, break the stitch down into these four motions:

1. Put the needle through the front of the stitch and out the back.
2. Wrap yarn around the needle.
3. Pull the new stitch through the old stitch.
4. Drop the old stitch.

Let new knitters practice knit stitches until they feel comfortable. You can show them how to cast-off in this lesson (if they are ready) and practice that on your swatch.

LESSON TWO: Review Lesson One. Show how to do a *backward cast-on* (which is the easiest cast-on), and let them practice the knit stitch, cast-on and cast-off, as they desire.

LESSON THREE: Review Lessons One and Two. Show how to make a purl stitch. Break it down into four steps. Be sure to note the difference in the first step between the knit and purl stitch.

For more information, go to these websites:

- Finger knitting:
  www.knitty.com/issuesummer06/FEATfingerknitting.html
- Kids' knitting needles and how-to information:
  http://pages.e-yarn.com/6030/PictPage/1922208403.html
  www.purplekittyyarns.com/index.asp?PageAction=VIEW
  PROD&ProdID=137

Party Time!

When Joey, age six, and Charley, four, come for their weekly visit to "Nana's" house, my friend Carol, an author and former columnist for a Chicago newspaper, throws a party. The boys usually come at about nine in the morning, so after they shoot a few baskets (in a big cardboard box Carol has placed strategically in her apartment) and play for a little while, she calls them to the table, set with festive placemats, animal-face paper plates, party hats, blowers, horns, and balloons. She serves "Mom-approved" organic milk (which the boys call *milk-shakes*) and small organic ginger-snap cookies, which are enough of a treat to delight the boys, but not so much as to spoil their appetite for lunch.

The party-atmosphere intimacy gives rise to lively conversations often started by the boys' questions: "Do you still have birthdays in Heaven?" "Why isn't Pluto a planet any more?" "How do you get a story in a newspaper?" They talk about their favorite colors, the animals on their plates, far-off countries—a wide gamut of topics. "I have learned so much from them; they told me more about the solar system than I told them," Carol says. "And there's so much I learn about how they think and how they see the world that I wouldn't know if we didn't have this special time together."

THROWING A GRANDKID PARTY

- If you live close enough to your grandchild so that you can see him or her often, setting up a regular time to visit builds anticipation between visits and makes the parties a high point in the child's life, as well, of course, as in yours. If not, party time can still, of course, be special for both generations.

- Encourage the child's parents to use party time to go out themselves, so you can have the grandkid all to yourself. You'll have a more intimate visit, as well as a happier one, since children *always* behave better when their parents are nowhere in sight.

- Buy special placemats, animal-face paper plates, and party favors at a drugstore, supermarket, or party store. Or get plain plates that children can decorate themselves. (Or use child-designed plates and mugs from Makit Products—see page 65.) Jump-start the conversation by asking simple questions about topics that interest your grandchild. If the subject interests the child, the conversation will take off from there.

$ $

And a Little Child
Shall Lead You

"Who cleans the rooms?" Rachel, age six, asked her grandmother, who had capped off their local visit to the Georgia Aquarium with an overnight stay at a nearby hotel. "Where do the rooms come from? How do you get to stay in the room?" Looking at the world through a child's eyes reminds us that so many things we adults never think about can lead to fascinating discussions and can give us a fresh viewpoint.

Discussions like this come up often during the local jaunts Maxine goes on with Rachel and, at other times, with four-year-old Julia. A major reason for the outings' success is that Maxine takes her cues from her grandchildren. The aquarium trip, for example, came up after Maxine and Rachel read stories in the Atlanta newspapers about its opening and then went to the computer to research the new attraction. A visit to a museum exhibit followed Julia's telling Maxine that her preschool class was studying the art of the kings of France. "She knew so much about the paintings and the furniture that it was more of an education for me than for her!" Maxine says. "It was like going with a small docent." And a classroom visit when Maxine talked about a book she had written about gorillas led to the Atlanta zoo to see gorillas up close and personal.

"I'm often surprised by the things the girls want to do," says Maxine. "And I'm always glad that I listen to them. You have to afford children the dignity of letting them take the lead. You don't have to make all the decisions."

PLAN PERFECT OUTINGS

Maxine points to other reasons for the success of these grandmother-grandchild excursions:

- She takes each child individually as often as possible. These one-on-one times together let them pursue the one child's own interests without being distracted by another child's desires. "When there is just one child and one adult, it's a more intimate experience for both," she says.
- She limits the trips to activities that will interest her as well as the children. "I don't go to any dumb stuff where I know I'll be bored," she says, adding that the children watch her expression closely to see if she's enjoying herself.
- She doesn't treat the excursions like an assignment, but takes her cue from the child. If the child's interest wanes, she drops any further reading or research. "I'm very hands-off," she says. "Children learn quite naturally if you leave them alone. And I want to be with a relaxed kid who can goof off."
- The wonderful thing about being a grandparent is that you don't need to teach the grandchildren all the things you already taught your own children. You can focus on just having a good time.

Presents, Presents, Presents

One time-honored grandmotherly privilege is the ability to spoil your grandchildren with lavish and endless gifts. So availing herself of this opportunity, my friend Bonnie (known as "Pally" to her grandchildren) enjoyed taking Nicky and Lexi on shopping extravaganzas. She would walk them into the store and tell them, "You can pick out anything you want, and I'll buy it for you." "Anything, Pally?" they would ask. "Anything at all," she would answer. This was easy on Bonnie's bank account, since she was not taking them to Neiman Marcus or F.A.O. Schwarz or even Toys "R" Us. No, Bonnie would take them to her local Goodwill store, soon to be known in the family as "Pally's Toy Store."

"We did this all the time," says Bonnie, a playwright in El Granada, California, "and they loved it—it was the ultimate luxury while it lasted." The low shelves were crowded with all sorts of toys that, new, are prohibitively expensive for most households. These excursions went on until the children turned about seven years old, and their mother pleaded with Bonnie, "Please—no more Barbie vehicles!"

Meanwhile, Bonnie began to explore other sources for presents for Nick and Lexi (now ages fourteen and thirteen), as well as for Lenny, now thirteen, and Angie, twelve, who live in Japan. She cruises the supermarket aisles for little toys and novelties, which sometimes include items like magnets, games to play in the car, bowl covers, and other odds and ends. "There are all kinds of little things that I might never think of if I didn't see them staring me in the face," Bonnie says. So she buys an assortment, makes up a care package, and ships it off.

BUYING PRESENTS THAT WON'T BREAK YOUR BANK

One great rule for buying grandkid presents is, the younger the child, the simpler (and less expensive) the present needs to be. Before Bonnie's grandchildren were born, she bought their layettes and later, their subsequent wardrobes—again, not at Saks Fifth Avenue, but at her local secondhand clothing store. "Just because I became a grandmother," she says, "doesn't mean that I got stupid! I could see that so many of these little clothes got outgrown before they ever got worn out, I took them home and washed them in my own machine, and they served perfectly."

Then, for pocketbook-friendly presents that will delight slightly older children, besides Goodwill and supermarkets, you can gladden toddlers' and preschoolers' hearts with a trip to your local office supplies store. At two, Nina adored sitting with me in my office and drawing on screamingly bright-colored Post-it notes before sticking them on herself, on me, on the floor, the file cabinets, on any surface in sight. Other sure-fire hits are staplers (especially novelty ones in animal shapes), Scotch tape dispensers (ditto), reinforcements, and of course, markers, colored pencils, notepads, and labels.

Other good places to find inexpensive presents are dollar stores, which often have toys, crafts, puzzles, jewelry, and other delightful items. Then there are flea markets, sometimes given the fancier name of *antique markets,* which yield great troves of treasures. The list of sources is endless, as are the hours of shared enjoyment in the shopping and the child's play that follow. Lori Jean gets rolls of nickels ($2) or dimes ($5), wraps them like "crackers," with ribbon on both ends, and hides them for the grandchildren to find. She recommends keeping a list handy for where you hid the rolls!

Sometimes the reason for a present is more important than the thing itself. When one of Barbara's eleven grandchildren celebrates a birthday, she takes the birthday child's siblings to a toy store so that they all can pick out gifts for themselves (with a pre-set dollar limit).

How Ya Gonna Keep 'Em Away from the Farm?

"I'm really retro," Patti says when talking about what she does with her six granddaughters, ages four to ten. "A lot of the things I do are the same things my grandparents did with me." But this granny is strictly twenty-first century. For one thing, she exemplifies the common situation these days of the "blended family": five of her granddaughters are offspring of her husband's children from a previous marriage. Furthermore, Patti combines the best of the old with the mind-set of the new.

So, on the one hand, when the girls come to visit Patti and her husband on their Indiana farm, they help to harvest raspberries and blackberries, and then make cobblers and jam, freezing for winter what they can't eat right away. In the kitchen, each girl wears an apron from Patti's apron collection that goes back over a century to her great-grandmother. "The minute they come in the house, they want to put on their aprons!" laughs Patti, "whether they'll need them or not."

On the other hand, Patti is the embodiment of a modern woman: She holds a full-time job as a nurse and then comes home to work the farm. She drives the tractor, plows, digs potatoes, and tells the girls, all city-dwellers: "You can be physical and can get just as dirty as you want, and then you can go in and get washed and changed and be a lady." The girls often go out with Patti to feed and water the cows and calves, and then come in for breakfast, which Patti serves on good china and silver settings, so they will learn how to set a "proper table"—and learn to use the right fork too.

THE BEST OF THE OLD—THE MIND-SET OF THE NEW

With fewer small family farms, visits to grandparents on the farm are rarer, but many of the activities Patti does with her granddaughters can be done anywhere, like the following:

- Five years ago, when they moved into the farmhouse, they let all the granddaughters make handprints on the wall of their mud room. Josie, age ten, points to hers and says, "Look how small my hand was!"
- On the next holiday, Patti plans to let the girls make paint footprints on the floor tiles. "After all, you get these handprints and footprints in a house anyway," she says. "This way, we all get to have some fun with them."
- "I'm not crafty," says Patti, "but I try to think of different things we can do together." She has taught the girls how to knit scarves, and she has gotten them started with other projects, like finishing the edging on fleece blankets.
- Patti and the girls look forward to their once-a-year outing to a nearby teahouse with its huge trunk full of fur boas and other dress-up items. "I try to expose them as much as possible to special things," Patti says. "Things they're not used to." They all enjoy their sandwiches and cookies dressed in borrowed finery, where they get a chance to use their good table manners.

$-$$

Never Too Late to Go to Camp

If you miss the summer camp activities you loved as a kid—or if, like me, you never went to sleep-away camp—you can go now, with your grandchildren. For the past two years, Laurie, her husband, their son and daughter-in-law, and Maya, age six, and Aidan, four, have slept in bunk beds at a rustic family camp near Yosemite National Park. "You have to be really adaptable to do this," Laurie says. "You need your flashlight to find the bathroom in the middle of the night, and you might even see a bear on the way." But many family camps have more grandparent-friendly amenities, like air-conditioned rooms with private baths and daily cleaning service. What they all have in common are a wide range of activities for a wide range of ages.

"Our grandkids love the coziness of it," says Laurie, "with everyone together in the same cabin. They also like the fact that we're all doing the same things—like making butterflies out of clothespins—so it's an equalizing kind of experience." And, of course, there are all those activities, including swimming lessons, dance lessons, marshmallow roasts, bingo, basketball and badminton, Ping-Pong, talent shows, and arts and crafts.

"Grandparents are in a wonderful position to offer children new experiences so that they can find niches for themselves that they might not find otherwise," Laurie says. For example, after going with her grandmother for burro rides at camp, Maya began taking horseback-riding lessons back in Santa Monica,

California, where her family owns a condo three miles from Laurie's home. "I think this would not have happened if we hadn't been at camp," says Laurie.

FINDING THE RIGHT FAMILY CAMP

Family camps represent one of the fastest-growing trends in the camping industry, with the numbers of camps offering family programs having doubled since 1995. Most run sessions for three to seven days, and the price typically includes accommodations (often a tent or a cabin, sometimes a room in a lodge), three generous meals a day (generally in a common dining hall), and almost all activities. A few pricey activities, like horseback riding, are sometimes extra. Prices range from $200 to $1,500 per person, often coming to under $1,000 for a whole family group, which makes them quite affordable. And both adults and children often welcome the opportunities to be with other people their own age, as well as each other.

If you don't have a wonderful personal recommendation for a specific camp, type "family camp" into your search engine. When I did this, I got 69 million entries! You can then narrow your search to your own part of the country, or a destination outside of the United States. Most camps now have websites, which give more information about their offerings, prices, availabilities, and so forth. Many camps have specialties, like music and arts (where everyone in the family can take a few lessons), water sports (sailing, kayaking, etc.), animals (including petting zoos), and so on. YMCA members get discounts at camps run by the "Y." As with any popular vacation option, it's good to apply well in advance, since the most popular and the most reasonably priced camps fill up quickly.

Become a Gingerbread Architect

*E*very Christmas for the past thirty years, Kate and her family have been getting together with two other families, now including Lucy, a year older than Kate's five-year-old grandson, Kai. Last year, Lucy, Kai, and their two-year-old brothers enjoyed a special project. Two weeks before the party, Kate pulled out the gingerbread-house kit she had used for her own son twenty years earlier (sometimes it pays to save!), and she and Kai made enough dough for two houses. Kate froze the dough and later baked the pieces. She baked two more houses, and after all the houses were assembled, the children decorated them with gumdrops, kisses, red licorice, jellybeans, small candy canes, and little figures of snowmen and tin soldiers.

The children spent two happy, absorbed hours at the party. The houses they decorated became centerpieces for family dinners throughout the holiday season, and all four children beamed with pride at their creations.

BUILDING YOUR GINGERBREAD HOUSE

If you have time to bake your own gingerbread, you and your grandchild will have a deliciously fragrant several hours' shared project. But if you don't have time to bake dough, cut out and assemble house pieces, and make icing, buy a pre-baked gingerbread house kit. These kits, available at crafts and hardware stores and online (search for "gingerbread house kit"), usually cost between $10 and $20. Typically, they include pre-baked gingerbread house pieces, icing mix, a plastic decorating bag and tip, assorted candies, and a cardboard base.

Here are some suggestions for making the houses:

- Buy extra candy because hard workers (including you) are likely to want to eat the decorations.
- Also buy other decorative items, like little figures, trees, square pretzels (which make good windows), and candy canes (for around the doors).
- Put the cardboard base onto a bigger piece of cardboard wrapped in tissue paper, to make the house easy to move.
- Depending on your grandchild's age, dexterity, and patience, you can either assemble the house together or do this ahead of time yourself. Mix the icing with water just before use, and use this mixture to glue the sides of the house together.
- Show your grandchild how to use the icing bag, and let him or her squeeze out the icing. Or use a small spatula to spread it. The house pieces have to set for at least an hour (more is better) before decorating.
- To make the candies stick, put soft icing on the bottom of each candy and hold it in place for a few seconds.
- If you'll be eating it over the next few days, wrap it in plastic wrap. The gingerbread is thick and may be hard on your teeth. Be careful!
- If you want to keep it for next year, spray with clear lacquer from the paint store, and keep it away from small children.
- For questions, go to **www.wilton.com**, a manufacturer.

Real Baking,
the Old-Fashioned Way

onnie, who takes care of her granddaughter in Arizona during the week while her daughter is at work, has introduced Mackenzie Grace (a.k.a. Kenz), age four and a half, to the delight of making healthy, delicious oatmeal cookies. The first time they did this together, Connie brought a child-size table into the kitchen, set a big bowl on it, and gave Kenz the ingredients, one by one.

Kenz's first task was to unwrap softened sticks of butter ("a waxy mess"). Then Kenz added the brown and white sugars (less than the amounts recommended in the recipe), meanwhile asking questions like, "What's the difference in the color, Nana?" Next came the creaming process, starting with a spoon and graduating to clean little fingers. Kenz cracked the eggs, managing to get most of them in the bowl, and then, with Connie's help, beat them and added them to the butter and sugar. Mmm . . . Kenz enjoyed sniffing the vanilla.

In a different bowl, she fluffed some flour with baking soda and some cinnamon. ("That's so funny that they call it flour, Nana. It doesn't even look like flowers.") Adding the three cups of oatmeal presented a challenge: "Nana, your turn, my hands are too tired."

GETTING A GREAT RESULT

Cooking with a small child is not for sissies. You have to be constantly on hand to fix glitches, like the dryness of Kenz's batter, since not all the eggs made it into the bowl. Connie added water, and she and Kenz made almost all the oats magically disappear. Kenz then used ice-cream scoops to measure out big balls of dough onto the cookie sheets. ("Not like the ones we sleep on!" she learned.) Report from Connie: The cookies were tasty—and, to no one's surprise, cleanup was a bit extensive. "But that's why paper towels were invented," she says, happy that they enjoyed "good ole-fashioned baking, without the colorful, expensive, prepackaged, hydrogenated, and preserved dough that advertises: 'So easy . . . kids can do it!'" Furthermore, the activity was a vocabulary builder—with Kenz learning new meanings for *flour* and *sheets*.

To succeed at baking with a grandchild, preparation is essential. Have all your ingredients and utensils ready, being sure they can be handled safely. Don't panic when the eggs go on the counter instead of the bowl, and flour decorates the floor. If you're likely to be upset by the mess, lay newspapers on the floor before baking. Plan the activity at a time when you're both full of energy: Little problems become big ones when either worker is tired! And if more than one child is baking with you, give each one enough to do so that no one is standing around without a job, primed to get into trouble.

Enjoy your cookies!

(Connie describes various activities she has done with Kenz on her blog, **www.playwitmenana.blogspot.com/**.)

$

She Finds Sea Shells

When four-year-old Grace comes to visit her Grammy, Ginny relives fun she had as a child. Now she and Grace walk the beach to find sea shells, label each one, and make plaques to keep or use as gifts. Ginny, who lives only five miles from the New Jersey shore, loves the hands-on aspect while exposing Grace to the many wonders in nature. And Grace loves all the stages of the project—her walks with Grammy, her treasure trove of shells, and the plaques she makes with them.

When Ginny and Grace bring their treasures back home, they carefully study each shell and look them up in Ginny's book, the Golden Nature Guide *Seashells of the World,* by R. Tucker Abbott. The 2001 updated version of this handy little book lists 600 different shells, is published by St. Martin's Press, and is available in both paperback and hardcover editions.

Then Ginny and Grace choose favorite shells to glue onto driftwood or cardboard to make plaques. So far Grace has made four, two of which she kept and two she gave as gifts. The tool that makes making plaques easier than in the past is a glue gun, available in art, crafts, and building supply stores. Ginny and Grace are right in step with the times, since women are the main users of these guns, whose use has grown over recent decades, from half a million sold annually to about 10 million today.

USING A GLUE GUN

When you go to buy a glue gun, tell store personnel what you plan to use it for, since the basic model has evolved into a wide variety of various sizes (some small enough to pop in your purse) and different functions, specialized for wood, glass, fabric, jewelry, and other items. Most cost $20 or less.

When using a glue gun with a child, you need to supervise him or her very carefully, since the glue can get as hot as 400 degrees Fahrenheit (204 degrees Celsius). Some glue gun users (like Christine Stickler, coauthor of *Wild with a Glue Gun: Getting Together with Crafty Friends*) consider bad burns to be an initiation rite, but you don't want your grandchild to go through this kind of initiation!

Before you attach your shells to the board, clean it carefully and sand it if it has a rough surface. You're less likely to get burned if you plunge your fingers in ice water before gluing your shells to the board, and if you can handle the shells with tweezers, toothpicks, or chopsticks.

A benign danger of using the glue gun is its versatility: Once you get used to using it for one project, like the sea shells, you may get hooked on using it for many purposes you never dreamed of.

Rainy Daze

"One of the best things I've ever done in my whole life was when we went out and walked in the rain," seven-year-old Zack said to Mary Ellen, remembering their adventure two summers earlier. While Zack was visiting his grandparents at the seashore, Mary Ellen was not about to let the sudden rainstorm dampen their spirits. She got out their rain boots, and both of them walked through the flooded streets, splashing in the deepest puddles, catching rain drops in their open mouths, and then, afterward, looking for rainbows. "With my own children," she says, "I used to let them walk barefoot in the rain, but since I didn't know how Zack's mother would feel about that, we played it safe and went out in boots."

Kate had an even more basic experience with her four- and two-year-old grandsons, this one *after* the rain when they sought out every mud puddle they could find. After walking and stomping, and then sliding in the mud and becoming part of the mud pie, she had to peel off their clothes before giving both them and their clothes a bath. "It was a fabulous afternoon!" she says. And Lenore adds her experience: "How many grandmas sit in the driveway and dig in the dirty sand and make roads for little cars and trucks? I do. But the real fun is when you add water to it and you make your castles and mud pies and get really dirty. My grandson and I had a ball; my daughter thought we were nuts."

Grandkids give us a second chance to be kids ourselves—to play and get messy and have fun doing it.

KEEPING KIDS BUSY ON RAINY DAYS

When all the equipment at the neighborhood playground is soaking wet and it's too cold to go outside in the rain, this is the time when you're glad you stocked up on games and craft activities or when you decide to embark upon cookie-baking or some other mildly messy indoor activity.

I always make sure that I have the ingredients for their favorite chocolate-chip cookies on hand, one old standby that's still popular in this digital age. I think the best recipes are the ones on the packages of chocolate chips. And, of course, cooking and baking in the kitchen gives kids and grannies another chance to get messy! After the baking is finished, it's time to pull a step-stool up to the sink and let your toddler or preschooler whip up loads of suds to wash all the pots and pans and non-breakable cups and plates. Your "helper" may even enjoy mopping up all the water that inevitably reaches the floor during the "cleanup."

Take Your Grandchild to Work

"When I was a little girl, my father regularly took me to work with him, and so it seemed like the normal and natural thing for me to take my children—and then my grandchildren," says Norma, president of a Harrisburg, Pennsylvania-based company that moves theatrical stage sets, props, and costumes. Since Norma and I became good friends at age fourteen, I came to know her father over the years and know how much he involved his children in the business. So it was not surprising when Norma's granddaughter, Sara, proudly announced at her Bat Mitzvah that Nana was holding a job for her, and that of all the grandchildren, she would be the one to run the company.

From the time that they were about three or four, Sara, her brother, and her cousins would go to the office with Nana, play with the copy machines, ride around the lot in the trucks, and just hang out to watch what was going on. "They got to see what we do, got to know the drivers and the office staff, and basically 'inhaled' a sense of the business," Norma says. As adolescents, some of the grandchildren did administrative tasks like answering the telephone, designing reports, and using the computer, and later on, have handled operations like dispatching drivers.

Not everyone, of course, can pass on a place in a family enterprise, but almost every working grandmother can give a grandchild a very special experience. More than thirty years later, one woman has warm memories of her visits to her grandmother's workplace. From the age of 11, Wendy would take two Philadelphia buses to visit her grandmother at the University of Pennsylvania. "Gram was in charge of the copy room in the chemistry department, and her job was to fill orders and maintain supplies to keep the department running," Wendy remembers. "This was back in the days of the 'ditto' machine, which copied everything to a lovely shade of purple. My sister and I could make up anything we wanted on a ditto-er, and Gram would let us crank out several whatevers so that we could give her one, give one to Mommy, and keep one for ourselves. It was so cool."

You never know which memories you will create. Among Wendy's treasured memories are her visits to Gram's friend, the glass blower, who made the beakers, distilleries, and glass widgets for the science projects. He also made the girls miniatures for their doll houses, vases, pitchers, and cups, treasures to take home after lunch with Gram. Norma's grandchildren, inspired by their early memories and by Nana's example, have gone on to continue the family business tradition.

IT'S OFF TO WORK WE GO!

The most important thing you can do to instill a feeling that work is fun, according to Norma, is to encourage your grandchildren to come to your workplace and have a good time there. Play is the work of children, and for children, work becomes play. Making copies or stapling papers can help young children see work as a satisfying way to spend time and a way to feel part of the larger venture. For one bakery plant operator, it was his childhood experiences baking pies with his grandmother that motivated him to continue in the family business. For the president of a billiard table company, it was listening to his grandfather's stories from the dark days of the Depression.

Your grandchildren can find inspiration from the history of your work life. Let them know how you got into your line of work, who influenced you, and what you experienced while starting out. Tell them stories—funny or dramatic. And above all, let them know that you will support their ambitions whether or not they choose to follow in your footsteps.

The School Years
(Ages Six to 11)

This is when another huge multi-capability growth spurt occurs in all aspects of a child's life. As you'll see in the following pages, you can be not only the beneficiary of this growth—you can help move it along and delight in the process. You can play games together, and who's to criticize you if in the process you make up your own rules? After all, you're the granny! You can pose challenges that lead to mastery of skills in sports, school, music, and logical thinking. You can show your grandkids that you care about them and are proud of them as you go to the important events in their lives: the Saturday morning soccer game under a light drizzle, the seemingly interminable gymnastics meet, the ballet recital with your tutu-wearing sweetheart in the back row, the school concert where some of the numbers are actually in tune. You can be their most appreciative audience.

And you'll be there at other times to talk about the emotional issues in your grandchildren's lives, to find out what's important to them, and to encourage their moral and psychological growth, along with the physical and the intellectual. These are the years when children look beyond their families,

*their friends, and their neighborhoods, and begin to think
about major concepts like justice and faith and caring for
others. Because you're not on the scene all the time, you can
be there at important times, and you can play a vital role in
their quests to find out the kind of people they want to be.*

Email to and from Anywhere

When Janet went to Southeast Asia under the auspices of a Christian mission whose work included helping survivors of the December 2004 tsunami, she was gone for three and a half months, a long time to be so far away from her nine grandchildren, back in Missouri. As often as she could, she communicated by email, especially with Andrea, age fourteen, who had specifically asked "Nano" (Janet) to email her at her computer at school, so that she could share with her classmates and her teacher Janet's emails about her work, some of which involved staying in the humble homes of Indonesians in Banda Aceh, helping to get a roof put on a village church, and founding a medical clinic.

"Our grandchildren are very fortunate, and I think it's good for them to learn how some people have to live. One of these days, we hope to bring each of our grandchildren here for a visit to experience the joy of helping people learn about God's great gifts," Janet says.

So many grandparents these days live far away from their grandchildren, and email offers a wonderful way to stay in touch. It's also handy even if you and the grandchildren live in the same town. You and they can email each other and pick up messages at times that are convenient for both of you. Email is informal and quick. It also lets you send photos easily.

A GUIDE TO SUCCESSFUL EMAILING

- Write about topics that interest your grandchildren. When I saw a movie recently with a long segment about Japanese rock music, I emailed Maika, my teenage granddaughter who has become interested in Japanese pop singers, told her a little about the movie, and asked whether it was playing near her home. I received an immediate answer (which isn't always the case).

- Send messages in different colors and type fonts, and change the size of type in various places for emphasis. You can create an initial cap, or set a whole paragraph in bold-face. My twelve-year-old granddaughter, Lisa, used to like to make every word a different color— you can too.

- Keep your messages short, especially for younger children. Young people don't have the patience to wade through a lengthy missive. Most older people don't either!

- Children often don't know what to write. In every email, ask one—and only one— question and ask them to write back with the answer. For younger children, ask about their favorite color, animal, or food. For older ones, ask about their activities, like "What moves are you doing in gymnastics?" "What kind of cookies did you sell with your scout troop?" or "How do you like your art teacher?"

- Learn how to use emoticons, those funny little cartoon-like pictures that you can insert to show happiness, disappointment, or surprise, for example, or to illustrate the topic you're writing about (like a birthday cake, a light bulb, a TV set, etc.). You can use your search engine to find "emoticons" and can download them for free.

- You can also make emoticons yourself by typing different keys. For example, you can make a smile with a colon, maybe a hyphen, and a right parenthesis :) or :-) so that when you turn your head sideways, you see a smiley face. Make a wink with a semicolon and a right parenthesis ;) or a sad face with a colon and a left parenthesis : (. Here are some emoticons that Lisa sent to me:

:-)	Smile	:-(	Frown
;-)	Wink	:-D	Laughing
:-P	Tongue-out (Lisa's favorite)		
:-<	Embarrassed	:-\	Undecided
=-O	Surprise	:-	Kiss
8-)	Cool (Lisa's other favorite)		
>:o	Yell	:-!	Foot in mouth
:'(	Cry	O:-)	Innocent
:-X	Lips are sealed		

- Email is a great way to contact more than one grandchild at once when planning an outing. Put everyone's email address in and send the date, time, and location for a play or other activity. Send a copy to parents of young kids.
- Send the grandkids URL (website address) links. When I come across an interesting website about art or animals, I send a clickable link. It's easy. I put my cursor on the URL in my web browser, click on "copy," and then paste it into an email.
- There are many animated websites that are *lol* (laugh-out-loud) funny. Ask your grandchildren to tell you what abbreviations they use. For example, *wbs* means "write back soon" and *bc* means "because."

- Have fun with emails. Choose playful fonts like Comic Sans. Change the size of type in various places for emphasis. Twelve-year-old Lisa used to love it when I made every single word a different color; yes, it's a little time-consuming, but worth it for her gleeful responses.

- Scan silly drawings or pictures from magazines and send them with emails.

- For young kids, the sillier, the better. Write multiple choice or true/false questions like: What did Granny do this morning? A) Ran a 26-hour marathon; B) Tickled Grandpa under his chin; C) Let all of the animals at the zoo out of their cages and brought home an elephant.

- Write emails on special, free cyber-stationery, which you can download from sites like **www.thundercloud.net**. There's background stationery for every special occasion you can think of, and the site offers tips on using it. Linda, who fosters German shepherd dogs, likes to write her emails on "paper" with paw prints.

- I find that I read the newspaper differently now that my grandchildren have email and that I can send them "clippings" by just a few clicks of my mouse. I just emailed an article about black squirrels to Lisa, who loves animals, one about teenage drivers to Maika and Anna and one about economics in Germany to Stefan.

- You can also email videos, either those you make yourself on your digital camera or funny ones you find on YouTube. The links to those are easy to send.

I think you get the message. Email is fun and a great way to keep in touch with the youngest generation!

Compose on the Keyboard

hen Nina, age six, was staying with us for a few days, she asked me to help her write a letter to her mom, who was attending an out-of-town meeting. In first grade, Nina is learning to read and write, and as you can see from the following, I didn't give her any help with composition, punctuation, or spelling. All I did was get her to the right screen on the computer. She took it from there and produced the following memorable prose. Will we have another author in the family?

- On Thanksgiving: "I am thankful for my family be ckos with out them I wouldn't be here."
- On the environment: "You should never put plooshin in the water be ckos it will ckill the fish be ckos we nent the fish too srviv my name is nina. I like fish be ckos I gost do."
- On her mom's multi-day business trip: "I miss my mommy so much I ckant evin thick a bawot hre."
- And the one I especially love: "I have a niaas Granmthr Hoo takcs kcare oav me she gens me evrethg I woat. I theike she is so nias to me. Othr then that I love hoars so much. She is 72 I am onle 6 to me that is a rele bige difrinsi."
- I suspect that she got some help from her teacher when her school submitted the following, which was published in her local paper under the heading, "*What the Holidays Mean to*

Me": "It means that families should celebrate holidays together on every single day which means now."

TO ENCOURAGE AUTHORSHIP

Children often want to express themselves from an early age. The key is not to force them to write; You don't want to make a chore of this. You can simply ask, "Do you want to write a story?" or "Do you want to write a letter?" or simply "Do you want to write on the computer?" The computer seems magical to many children, and those who might have trouble with coordination and making legible letters will find it much easier to express their thoughts through the keyboard. Even children who don't have this trouble will find that the writing can go faster and neater when they type. You don't even need a computer; you can often get the same kind of result by hauling out your old type-writer. Here are some pointers to encourage enjoyment and creativity:

- Don't tell your grandchild what to write. If she asks you, try asking, "What do you want to write about?" If she says she doesn't know, maybe you can suggest a topic, like a letter to Santa Claus, a letter to her teacher, a letter to a relative in another city, and then let her say what she wants to.
- Don't correct spelling, grammar, or punctuation. This is not a school exercise or homework. If your grandchild asks you how to spell something, ask him, "How would you spell it?" and if he comes up with his own version, let it be. But if he does want your help, of course you can give it to him.

Start Conversations

These days, when so many children and teenagers spend so much of their time watching television or text-messaging on their cell phones, we often have to make a special effort to have times when we can have a conversation we all can enjoy. One of the nicest times during a recent visit to my daughter, Jenny, and her children, who live in Germany (and therefore we don't see each other as often as we all would like), was the lively conversation we had during a three-hour train trip. We talked about our three-day visit to Berlin, what we liked doing there, what our high points were (we didn't get around to low points, although they're important, too). Then somehow we got on to the subject of earliest memories, which everyone enjoyed talking about. Lisa, age ten, remembered being about four years old and standing in front of her sister's large bird cage and seeing her sister holding a baby dove. Maika, eighteen, had a memory going back earlier to age two and a half, when she was sitting in her crib and looking at colored plastic blocks, which were in a box underneath the crib. She wanted to play with them but could not reach them.

A good way to start a conversation is to watch a TV show or a movie with your grandchildren, and then use that as a jumping-off point to talk about topics raised by the show. It could involve bullying, violence, cheating, or many other issues that, if raised independently, might sound like moralizing.

GOOD TOPICS

These are some good topics of conversation with children of different ages:

- Where do you go when you want to be alone?
- What do you do if you're angry with a friend?
- How do you make up with a friend after an argument?
- Who are three famous people you would like to have as friends?
- What is your biggest dream?
- What is your favorite subject in school?
- What is your least favorite subject?
- Who is your favorite teacher? Why?
- Who is your least favorite teacher? Why?
- What kinds of things do you think are unfair?

Rediscover Childhood Games

When my cousin Debbie, a teacher of English as a second language, was a child, she loved to play Monopoly with her cousins, and now she is playing the game again, this time in the junior version, with her six-year-old grandson, Guy.

"This is a terrific activity," she says, "because it gives Guy a lot of attention, and he learns arithmetic at the same time. The bank gives each player so much money, and sometimes you run out of ones, and then you have a five-dollar bill, but you only have to pay $3. So Guy has to figure out the subtraction, and he learns while he's having fun."

In one game, Debbie was winning, and Guy was left with only a couple of dollars, not enough to keep playing. As Guy saw that he was going to lose and the game would end, his sadness was obvious. "I didn't want to forfeit," Debbie says. "I think that they have to learn to play by the rules, as they will have to play with other children by the rules." So Debbie saved the day by saying, "Look, Guy, I am a grandma, and grandmas have privileges. They can give their grandchildren birthday money (even if the birthday is months away!)." Debbie gave Guy $5 in Monopoly money so that he could have some "capital" and continue the game. He was thrilled, and two days later, Debbie found the $5 bill folded neatly into one of his little notebooks. It was clear that his "birthday" money meant so much to him, and Grandma and Guy had their little secret.

FINDING GAMES

A trip to any bookstore, toy store, or garage sale will offer a bounty of games, many of which you will recognize from your childhood or your children's younger years. Remembering when you played Candyland with your own preschoolers, you may want to travel the roads again with your grandchildren. Or you might opt for some other family favorites or even child-oriented versions of adult games that you enjoy playing with your adult children or your friends, like Junior Scrabble.

The important thing is that you orient the game to your grandchild's age and interest, and that you enjoy playing yourself. If you are doing this as a chore, you won't have a good time, and neither will your grandchild. Sometimes it's hard for us adults to forget our everyday concerns and pressures long enough to take the time to play, but I know that whenever I have done it, I've been happy I did.

Many games can now be played on computer, but one problem with playing online is that you can't change the rules or improvise (like, for example, lend a grandchild the money he needs to keep up with the game), and in our family, we include preschoolers in our game playing by developing idiosyncratic rules for younger players. For example, in Pictionary, a game in which teams take turns drawing items on cards and then guessing what the drawing is, we skip the harder words and just pick another card. And when only a grandmother and grandchild are playing, we just draw the pictures without being competitive.

Hunt for Treasures

When my friend Sue, communications manager for an international professional services firm, was growing up in Columbus, Ohio, she and her friends used to play "Treasure Hunt." Recently, Sue harked back to her own childhood and created a treasure hunt for two of her grandchildren, Ruby, then age eight, and Benny, eleven.

After the treasure hunters tracked down all the rhyming clues, there it was in all its splendor: a glittering mound of riches. Ruby and Benny gazed upon silver and gold and jewels—bracelets and necklaces and rings, pins (one shaped like a scimitar to lure the most macho young treasure hunter), elegant-looking watches that hadn't told time for eons, and souvenirs of trips to the Eiffel Tower, the Statue of Liberty, the Golden Gate Bridge, and ethnic markets from around the world.

What better use for all those tchotchkes we haven't worn or looked at for years—if ever—but somehow haven't been able to part with? Sue's precious hoard finally found happy takers, as Ruby and Benny went through each and every item, turned it over, talked about it, and ended up taking whatever they wanted. As soon as the last bit of loot had been shared, Ruby asked, "Can we do the hunt all over again?" even though she now knew all the clues.

"It was a roaring success," Sue told me. "It was like in the movies, when you see the gang of tomb raiders burst through an underground cavern and find the booty. If you could have seen their faces when they lifted that pillow and found all that gold!"

CREATE A TREASURE HUNT

- Draw a map (of your home, your grandchildren's home, your backyard, etc.—wherever you want the hunt to take place) to find the treasure.
- Carefully burn it at the edges until it looks authentic enough to lure the most skeptical treasure seeker.
- Age the map by staining it with tea, pouring grease on it, and wrinkling it.
- Write out ten clues on little pieces of paper, directing the treasure hunters to different hiding places in your home (piano bench, magazine rack, under a bed, and other good spots, with levels of difficulty gauged to ages of the children).
- On every paper, write the number of the clue.
- Make the final clue the easiest one: maybe under the pillow on your bed.
- Leave the paper clues at each of the locations you have selected for the children to find. The first one, for example, might be under a rug by the front door.
- The second could be on a child's-eye-level bookshelf in your linen closet.
- And so on until the children have found the treasure.
- A sample clue could read like this: "(2) Ding dong, come to dinner, Bing bong, you're a winner. 20 paces" (The hiding place is under the dining-room table.)
- Milk and cookies for the weary treasure hunters are in order now!

Teach Your Grandchild
to Cheat "Honestly"

*Y*oung children hate to lose in any game. And although it's not a milestone we brag about, the ability to cheat is a major cognitive advance. Your little darling is wising up. He realizes that he is no longer at the mercy of the deal of the cards, the roll of the dice, and luck in general. He can now be master of his own fate, at least while playing a game. So what's a granny to do?

When my friend Karin's eight-year-old granddaughter began to cheat in the card and board games they played together, Karin made a game of it: "Okay, let's play one game *with* cheating and another *without* cheating." The game with cheating worked fine, but all too often the one without cheating ended in the little girl's tears, the grandmother's frustration, and an abrupt end to the game—and the playful mood.

Then, on a trip, Karin learned a new card game, which she adapted and renamed "Stinker" (because the name she learned for it was too vulgar!). In this game, children can cheat "honestly," or, as it's known in poker, can "bluff." I played "Stinker" with ten-year-old Lisa, who loved it. Besides being fun, it helps children learn to read other people's expressions and body language, advancing their social skills.

RULES FOR PLAYING "STINKER"

- Any number can play.
- Everyone is dealt seven cards.
- The object of the game is to get rid of all your cards.
- Whoever has an ace starts the game, which then goes clockwise.
- If no one has an ace, whoever has a two starts out, and so forth.
- Taking turns, every player lays a card facedown on the table in consecutive order but without regard to suit. That is, you can play an ace of hearts, a two of diamonds, a three of spades, and so on.
- Each player has to say which card she is putting down (for example, a two of spades, a three of clubs, or a king of hearts).
- If a player does not have the next number in order, she can draw a card from the deck.
- Or she can cheat by putting down a card that is not the right one but saying it is.
- If another player suspects that the current player put down the wrong card, he can challenge by calling out, "Stinker!"
- If the player put down the right card, the challenger has to pick up whatever cards have already been played and also draw one from the deck. If the player is caught cheating, she has to pick up the cards and draw one.
- The first player who plays all the cards in her hand wins, and (if more than two are playing) play continues until only one player is left with cards.

Arty Birthday Poems

From the time Mollie and her brother were very young, everyone in their family wrote rhymes to each other for birthdays and holidays. Now Mollie uses new computer tools to write illustrated poems for her four grandchildren.

The rhymes are all personalized, as in, "Chana, you've reached the age of nine and I'm so glad you're one of mine, with caring eyes and shining hair, which you've grown long because you care." (Chana's decided to donate her locks to a charity that gives wigs to children with cancer.) On Miriam's sixth birthday: "I hope your life is filled with love and dreams, I hope you can go fishing in some very sparkly streams." To Nachum on his twelfth: "Reading, playing, scouting, praying, oh you do them all so well. You're a good brother to your sisters (when you're not, I'll never tell!!!)." For Esti, at 14: "May you always keep sparkling like a bright star, may you always aim high, never feel it's too far."

Mollie emails the rhyme the night before the birthday and alerts the child's parents to print it out and hang it in the kitchen the next morning. "It's always an adventure to read the signs and poems hanging on the wall or fridge or door," she says, "because everyone who can hold a crayon or marker does one or two or three for every birthday, and each household makes a big fuss about the first viewing of all the Scotch-taped papers, and everyone reads them over and over again, pointing out their favorite bits."

What makes the poems especially beguiling (aside from having a custom-written greeting, often in the rhythm of a familiar song) is the way they're illustrated with little pictures tailored to the text. Here's where the computer comes in again.

CLIP ART TO THE RESCUE

You don't have to be an artist to illustrate poems or letters to your grandchildren. You just have to discover clip art. This is a catch-all term for images that you can find on the Internet and can download into your document. Much of it is public domain, but even if it carries some kind of copyright, no one is going to sue you for using it to wish your grandchild a happy birthday! If you don't have clip art in your word processing program, you can locate images by typing "clip art" into your search engine.

After Mollie composes her poem using MS Word, she puts her cursor near a noun she wants to illustrate, clicks on "Insert", then "Select Picture," then "Clip Art." To illustrate the word *exercise,* she sets clip art to: "Search," "Search in all collections," "All Media Types." She clicks a picture, adjusts the size, and there she is! "Finding the right pictures takes more time than the poem," she says. Many drawings and photos (including your own) come up, and you can work with them or change the term you want to illustrate. Finally, Mollie formats her poem and chooses font, size, and color.

"Anyone can learn to do this," reassures Mollie. She suggests starting by rhyming cheer and year, birthday and mirth day, boy and joy, girl and whirl, or not rhyming at all. "The message you want to send is, you matter, you count, and you are loved. We all need that message."

Help with Homework

When eight-year-old Chelsey was staying for a few days with Grandma Francine in Melbourne, Florida, Chelsey had an assignment to read and report on a book about Ben Franklin's early years. As Chelsey read aloud, Francine, a business consultant, was fascinated by the "then" versus the "now." "All the things I took for granted," she says, "were light-years away from Ben's experiences." So she suggested that as part of Chelsey's homework, they re-create ("as much as reasonably possible!") what it was like in young Ben's world.

"I had no salt pork, smoked ham, fresh fish—or huge open hearth for cooking," says Francine. So among leftovers in the fridge, they chose food that seemed closest to what young Ben might have eaten—fruits, cold meat, and dark bread—which they served on wooden planks. When darkness began to fall, they took a walk, lighting their way with candles, and word games replaced TV and DVDs.

Then, as they sat outside, Chelsey giggled and exclaimed as Francine told ghost stories, using her best "really scary" voice and waving one arm. (The other held tight to the candle.) Both Chelsey and Francine were utterly lost in the moment, Chelsey had her report, and Francine reports that "that bond, that connection between us, was indescribable."

HOW TO HELP

Bringing the perspective of another generation can often provide a fresh slant to a homework assignment and can turn work into play for both parties. To become a homework coach, let your grandchild's parents know that you are available, and tell them what subjects you are particularly interested in, and able to help with. If you are an accountant or bookkeeper, for example, you may be ideally suited to help with real-life math problems.

Ask and They Shall Receive

What would she like? What would delight him? How to find out? Sometimes it's hard to know what our grandchildren would like to do when they come to visit us or we go to see them. This is especially hard when, as is so often the case these days, the generations live far apart. However, email and cheap phone plans do make it easier.

A couple of months before my ten-year-old granddaughter, Maika, was due to come with her mother and sister from their home in Germany for their annual visit to us in the United States, I wrote to Maika to ask her to send me a list of what she would want to do or see when she came. Some of her requests were very modest (like getting books from the library, taking walks, and sleeping at her aunts' houses), while others required a little more effort—and expense (seeing the Empire State Building, the Bronx Zoo, and *The Lion King* on Broadway). Having the list gave us a good basis for planning her visit.

I wrote back to tell her which of her requested activities she would definitely be doing, and then said, "You may not have time to do all the other things on your list, so maybe you should write them down in the order of how important they are to you." She rank-ordered her desires, and we did manage to cover most of them, and to save a couple of items for the next visit.

FILLING REQUESTS

Few of us are mind readers, so it's always good to get as much feedback as possible about children's own wishes for what they want, as opposed to making plans based on what *you* think they will want. Although some attractions retain their appeal over the generations (like the zoo and shopping excursions), your grandchildren will not necessarily want to do the same things that your children enjoyed at the same age. For one thing, each child has his or her own unique personality. And for another, what twenty-first century children want is often very different from what a child would have wanted twenty or thirty years ago. So it pays to ask! These days, email makes the asking and answering much easier, and is better than a phone request because the children have a chance to think about what they want, and then you have the list in writing.

Before we bought the pricey tickets for *The Lion King,* we had asked our daughter and the children whether this was something they wanted to see. Their enthusiasm made the outlay seem worthwhile—and it was! The afternoon was a huge success, as were several of the other activities Maika had put on her list. (There have been other less successful times when we made plans without checking first, and ended up with crankiness all around.)

We do need to give ourselves an out just in case your grand-child's desires run to delights that would fit the wallet of a hedge fund manager, the energy level of an Olympic athlete, or the time availability of a playboy. So we have to tell them that while we will fulfill as many requests as possible, asking for something doesn't necessarily mean getting it! This is an important lesson to learn early in life.

Stand Up for Your Beliefs

When I first met Harriette, we both lived in suburban Chicago, we both had small children, and we were both active in the civil rights movement, taking part in civic actions and public marches and vigils to fight discrimination in housing. Harriette went on to write award-winning children's books about African American characters living at times of actual historical events. She also went on to become the grandmother of four.

One recent cold, blustery evening, eleven-year-old Conrad looked at a group of people standing in front of a church near Harriette's house in Oak Park, Illinois, and asked, "Grammy, why are those people standing there?" Harriette explained that these people believed that the nation should not be at war and that they stood at that spot every week to bring public attention to their cause. "Can we stand with them?" Conrad asked. So Harriette stopped the car, they joined the group, and that evening was a major event in Conrad's life as he stood with his grandmother and with other people who were willing to withstand the biting wind for their beliefs. His time in the cold was warmed by the lively music—old songs like "Give Peace a Chance" sung to flute and drums—as he experienced the rallying force of committed people singing and standing together.

INVOLVING GRANDCHILDREN IN PUBLIC LIFE

As Harriette says, "The important thing is to help your grand-children develop their value systems and to let them see that being American means more than having your own car and going out partying." We have many opportunities to share our values with our grandchildren.

We can take them with us on a march or a vigil. We can enlist their help stuffing envelopes or giving out flyers for a political mailing. We can suggest that when they feel strongly about a public issue, they write a letter to the editor of the newspaper. Before Conrad was even in school, he watched his grandparents and his father set up mattresses at churches and a synagogue to offer shelter to homeless people. Harriette's family abides by the motto: "Think globally, act locally." In today's complex society, there's no shortage of issues with which children can become involved.

Go the Distance

"Here we were on a 900-mile (1,448-kilometer) drive with our twelve- and nine-year-old grandchildren, and I never once heard the words I used to hear from my own children: 'Are we there yet?'" says Pauline. Since Sara and Christopher's parents could not attend that year's family get-together, Grandma Pauline and Grandpa Dudley drove the children from their home in St. Paul, Minnesota, to Estes Park, Colorado.

It was an easy decision for the grandparents: If they had not driven, the children would not have been able to spend the week in the park with three of their cousins, as well as uncles, aunts, and grandparents. And that would have been too bad. With the families spread out among Minnesota, Montana, and Colorado, these annual get-togethers have become important to all the children, as well as to the parents and grandparents.

Highlights of the week included all five children piling into one bedroom, climbing rocks in the park, Christopher's catching his biggest trout ever, and cousins Sara and Hayley cooking three-bean chili stew and flan with Grandma. "It's so nice to sit back and look at the younger generations and see that all is well," Pauline says. And Hayley expresses the feelings of her generation: "We always look forward to it so much; it's really special being with my grandmother because we don't get to see her that much." Being together for an entire week provides time for relaxed conversations, and Pauline, a professor and family therapist, talks with the children about options for their future, the book she's currently writing, and how they're doing in, and out of, school.

BEING THERE AND GOING THERE FOR THE GRANDCHILDREN

"Some grandparents are shy about saying, 'I'm available' or 'I want to do this,'" says Pauline. But an important role for grandparents is to do what parents may not be able to do themselves. Thus, when Erin, age fourteen, had a special opportunity to study in France, Pauline and Dudley escorted her there and made time for quality one-on-one time. "We had some good talks," Erin says, "about France, about books, and about psychology. Grandma has modern ideas, not at all old-fashioned."

You need to emphasize to your children that they have to let you know far enough ahead when your help is wanted. We modern grandparents have busy lives ourselves and are often unable to pitch in on a moment's notice (except for emergencies, of course—when we *always* make time). Pauline's daughter, Ann, says, "I try to plan well in advance so that if we want or need her to do something, she can put it on her calendar."

Today's calendars are likely to be electronic, and cutting-edge technology can make grandparenting easier in many ways. Pauline's grandchildren, for example, had packed their own entertainment: handheld computers stocked with electronic games and CD players for favorite music, along with old standbys like puzzles and books. The result: total immersion and concentration. In our car, my grandchildren sometimes listen to children's books on cassettes or CDs or music on MP3 players, and even watch movies on a DVD player. (All of these gizmos make terrific grandparent gifts.) Then, of course, there are the time-tested aids for car rides, like frequent stops to get out and walk around (and, on Pauline's road trip, get used to increasing altitude so that the 9,000-foot [2,743-meter] heights in the park would not cramp anyone's style), eat at roadside truck stops, visit local sights and museums, and break up the trip with an overnight motel stay.

Share Your Passions

My friend Mickey, a social activist in Cleveland, adores the theater, New York City, and her family—not necessarily in that order. As often as she can swing it, she jets into New York for theater marathons, and when each of her grandchildren turned eight, she began sharing her passions with them, one lucky child at a time.

Here's Mickey's routine: She flies from Cleveland to Washington, D.C., where her grandchildren, Alexandra and Benjamin, live; picks up the designated child; and rides Amtrak with him or her to New York's Pennsylvania Station. They stay for two nights at the time-share that Mickey and her husband, Al, own, just blocks from the theater district. Before each trip, she researches Broadway and Off-Broadway offerings, which so far have included such child-and-granny-pleasers as *The Lion King* and *Blue Man Group*; she also takes them to museums chosen for the child's special interest of the moment; and she seeks out other activities like the big Ferris wheel at the Times Square Toys "R" Us store. Benjamin's biggest hit on his first trip wasn't Broadway, though; it was a serendipitous outing that started with a public bus ride and ended in Washington Square Park, where he sat down with one of the men who play chess with all comers, two games for five dollars, and he learned some new strategies. Not everyone, of course, can afford to treat a grandchild to a theater weekend in Manhattan, but New York, like most cities, offers a wide range of free and low-cost children's and adult offerings, which put a much smaller dent in a grandmother's budget. And grandmothers have many other passions that they can share with their grandchildren.

PLANNING A GRANDCHILD'S WEEKEND

Whatever your passion—dance, hiking, animals, art, or anything else—share it. Ideally, share it with one child at a time, for very special one-on-one time. You don't have to go far: An hour's drive or train ride to a nearby town, with a night or two spent in a modest hotel or motel, will give a special gloss to your adventure.

Doing just a little planning ahead of time will help the two of you get the most out of your weekend. Most cities, even small ones, have websites where they advertise special attractions. If New York City is your destination, go to **www.nycvisit.com** to plan your time. Also check out *Frommer's New York City with Kids,* by Holly Hughes. But suppose you want to go someplace smaller and nearer—say, Frederick, Maryland. Just type the name of your destination town into your search engine, and voilà!: **www.fredericktourism.org** offers you a wide selection of activities.

Before you embark on your first trip together, it's a good idea to have your grandchild spend an overnight at your home, so you'll get a feel for each other's rhythms, and you'll see how comfortable the child is about spending time away from home. When you're ready for your trip, you'll want your grandchild to be in on the planning. You can make suggestions, but let the child pick the ones that appeal to her. You can sometimes make a deal, too, as I did once with my teenage granddaughter, Maika: I promised to take her to a store she was dying to go to and to spend as much time as she wanted, on the proviso that she go with me to a museum I wanted to see (and wanted her to see too). She agreed, we were both satisfied, and we both had a great time.

On the River with Granny

On his first white-water rafting trip, Ryan, age eight and a half, told his 83-year-old grandparents, "Even if I die, this is the best vacation ever!" Of course, Ryan didn't die, or even get injured, since strict safety standards were practiced on the river, and a good time was had by all.

Helen and Ed took their four children, one daughter-in-law, and three grandchildren (Ryan, Drew, age nine, and Heather, eleven) for a five-day trip on Idaho's Salmon River. They flew from New Jersey to Denver, then to Boise, then on a ten-passenger, two-propeller plane to the tiny town of Salmon, where they spent one night. From there, it was five nights in back-country lodges and four days on the river, where some in the group kayaked, some paddled rafts, and some relaxed while the guides paddled.

When Arnella took her grandchildren from Arizona on the same kind of trip, they slept in tents or in the open, seeing the stars as they never could at home, after enjoying evenings around the campfire. "Besides a wonderful adventure," she said, "I was amazed at what outstanding meals were served with such limited facilities." One dinner included asparagus wrapped in ham, roast beef, king crab legs, and strawberry-chocolate dessert.

In addition to the excitement of fording rapids on a wilderness river, these "river rats" made stops to pan for gold, visit a trading post, explore a homestead that once housed a slave who had been won in a card game, sunbathe on a beach, soak in a hot spring, and view Indian pictographs. Idaho Grandma Pat's eleven-year-old grandsons loved their river adventure "and would be happy to go every summer." "If an opportunity like this ever arises," says Pat, "go for it!"

FUN AND SAFETY ON THE RIVER

"A high point for me," says Helen, "was watching all of them having fun! We had looked forward to a family adventure such as this for several years, but had to wait for the boys to be old enough. Our own age was not a problem—we had gone on our first rafting trip at age 74—and enjoyed this big adventure nine years later even more."

Both Arnella and Helen took their white-water trips with Dave Warren's Warren River Expeditions, Inc. (**www.Raft Idaho.com**). Dave, whose motto is "Idaho is what America used to be," operates a variety of river trips and says, "An intergenerational lodge trip allows you to spend time with your family and grandkids without all the interruptions of the outside world. You get the excitement of the white-water rafting without having to rough it." Children should be at least six years old, but there's no upper age limit! Like other reputable rafting outfitters, Dave emphasizes safety and the need to adhere to the rules of the river. He also provides rafters with a list of the items they'll need for the trip, and places to buy them if necessary.

Other outfitters operate in other parts of the United States and in other countries. Mark and I have gone on—and loved—white-water trips in Idaho, California, the Grand Canyon,

Costa Rica, and Peru (none yet with our grandchildren). To find an outfitter for your destination, type into your search engine "river rafting" and the geographical area that interests you. When you find one who sounds good, ask for references from people who have traveled with the outfitter, and be sure all the guides are licensed and know first aid, as well as river safety. And once you're set, follow Dave's advice to bring lots of extra clothes for the younger kids. "That way," he says, "when they get wet—and they will—there isn't a fuss about getting their only set of warm clothes wet."

$ $$ $$

Wii—WHEE!

Since Carolyn lives just twenty minutes away from her grandchildren, they come to see her about once a week at Sedgebrook, her retirement home in Lincolnshire, Illinois. They never have to worry about what to do on a visit now that they can all play with the Nintendo Wii (pronounced "we") video games. When Jonathon, age eight, and Jessica, twelve, saw Carolyn's fellow residents "bowling" via the Wii on a huge-screen TV, they said, "Let's sign up for that!"

The children, who had already played with the Wii at friends' houses, set about teaching Grandma how to manipulate the buttons on the handheld remote controller, and since then, bowling and boxing with her are high points of their visits. Their games usually last about an hour and a half. ("They'd last longer if Grandma held up," laughs Carolyn.) Wii games can be strenuous, with players moving their bodies the same way they would if they were playing an actual game rather than a virtual one. Thus, bowlers crouch the same way they would in a bowling alley, pull back their arms, and release the ball using the same motions. With the Wii, they have to push the button on the controller at the precise time they let go of the ball. Flora, another Sedgebrook resident, told me that her four-and-a-half-year-old grandson bowled 112 with the Wii, and Flora was the first to bowl a 300 game in a Sedgebrook tournament. One senior resident called the Wii a "grandchild magnet," which encourages kids to visit their grandparents. It's the first video game that has gone social, in which families and friends play it together.

PLAYING WITH THE Wii

To play with the Wii at home, you need the video game console with its wireless controller, the Wii Remote. You hold the remote in your hand and strap it loosely to your wrist so that you can't drop it. Then you point it at your video screen, move your arm, and push the button according to whatever game you are playing. As of this writing, the basic Wii equipment, with one or more games, costs about $250. Then you can buy an amazing variety of additional games, some for very young children.

My granddaughter and I had a good time with the "Carnival" game set: twenty-five games, like the ones you would find at a fair, which up to four players can play: Ring the Bell to Test Your Strength, Alley Ball, Ring Toss, Balloon Darts, Clown Splash, Shooting Gallery, and so forth. You rack up points and even get virtual prizes (without having to clutter up your grandkids' shelves with more stuffed animals). You and your grandchildren can also practice tennis, fishing, golf, baseball, or other skills with the appropriate games.

You can also play poker. But my high school classmate Ricky, who learned "Texas Hold-'em Poker" from her grandchildren in Eugene, Oregon, prefers the card-holding kind over the Wii. When they played the Wii version, she was impressed by how well three-year-old Macy could manipulate her remote—"a lot better than I could!" Ricky confessed.

One plus for seniors using the Wii is its popularity in rehab therapy for patients recovering from surgery, broken bones, and other conditions. Enthusiasts call it, "Wii-habilitation." But some orthopedists warn against "Wii-itis," the equivalent of tennis elbow. So the message seems to be, like everything else, Wii-moderation is the key.

How Does Your Garden Grow?

*E*very fine day between late spring and early fall, Mitzi is out in her vegetable garden in the small town where she lives in Hessen, Germany. Twenty years ago, when her eldest granddaughter, Elena, was small, Oma Mitzi began to take her into the garden with her. When Maika and then Lisa (my granddaughters too) came along, Mitzi initiated them into the world of growing things.

Mitzi enjoyed helping the girls in the garden, especially since her own two sons and two grandsons expressed little interest in it as children. For each granddaughter, she would set aside one small patch for the child's plants, and she would maintain the rest of the garden herself. (In between the girls' gardening forays, Mitzi maintained their patches too.) It has generally worked out that Mitzi gardened with one grandchild at a time, since each girl's interest has been highest in early grade school. As the girls got older, other activities have claimed their attention. This worked out well, giving Oma precious one-on-one time with each granddaughter.

When interest has been high, Maika and Lisa have planted cherry tomatoes, zucchini, beans, onions, and scallions, watered them, and harvested them. One successful crop is radishes, which ripen quickly and can be planted every two weeks. Furthermore, they need a great deal of water, thus providing an appealing activity on hot days. Lisa always enjoyed collecting bugs, worms, and especially, centipedes, which she liked holding in her hand. The girls' hands-down favorite activity has been harvesting strawberries. They would take a bucket, walk carefully between the rows, and pick the ripe berries. Mitzi laughs as she remembers how many of the strawberries found their way into eager mouths. "I was always happy when they came, and I enjoyed working with them," she says.

GARDENING WITH GRANDCHILDREN

You can now pursue the age-old activity of gardening with the up-to-the-minute resources of the Internet. One wonderfully informative website, maintained by the National Gardening Association, is **www.kidsgardening.com**. Click on "Parents' Primer" and access ten chapters by Cheryl Dorschner about gardening with children.

Chapter One, "Gardening at Every Age," confirms Mitzi's awareness that children's interest in gardening varies at different ages, and it suggests activities for each age (like blowing the fuzz off dandelions for preschoolers). "Turning Kids On" offers suggestions, many of which Mitzi followed intuitively: She showed the grandchildren how much she loved gardening by "reveling" in her own garden every day, she respected their capabilities and attention span and didn't demand more than they wanted to give, and she did behind-the-scenes maintenance of the girls' own vegetable patches on days when they didn't come to the garden. "Plants Kids Will Love" suggests putting in "performing plants" like ferns that close to the touch, wild plants like milkweed and thistles that attract butterflies, and extreme plants like huge sunflowers and tiny cherry tomatoes.

Other chapters deal with such topics as safety, themes, and design. The site also sells products like bright-colored child-sized tools, the "Pollinator Field Journal" that teaches about bees and hummingbirds, and "10 Terrific Vegetables," a book and seed collection.

Googling "gardening with children" will bring up other helpful websites as well, like www.eartheasy.com/grow_gardening_children.htm and www.urbanext.uiuc.edu/firstgarden.

Music, Music, Music

*A*ll five of Lerotha's grandchildren have gravitated toward the arts, and they have all inherited her musical talent. In addition to being an inspiring role model, she encourages them in other ways. A soprano who has sung professionally in such diverse venues as Tanglewood, Massachusetts, and Salzburg, Austria, Lerotha remembers the first song she sang in public at the age of seven (the old one about mother that starts out, "M is for the million things she gave me"). Lerotha's grandchildren have begun studying music at about the same age, and one way she spurs them on is by giving them their own professional status.

When Lerotha was asked to sing at a wedding reception and after the bride said she didn't have an accompanist, Lerotha said, "I have a grandson who can play with me." (As Lerotha told me, "Sometimes you have to push for your grandkids.") And so Reginald, age fourteen, got his first professional gig. The two of them practiced a few times, at the reception Reginald played his violin while Lerotha sang the "Lord's Prayer" and other songs, and at the end of the evening, she gave him half of her honorarium. Reginald now plays with the Montgomery County Youth Orchestra and will go to Japan with it next year. At other times, Lerotha has given small amounts of money to her musical grandchildren, including Reginald's sisters, Lydia, age twelve, and Sarah, seven, after performances. "They won't get rich this way," she says, "but they'll see that their playing has value in addition to the pleasure they get from it."

By encouraging her grandchildren's musicianship and enjoyment of classical music, Lerotha is doing her best to answer the question from someone at a music festival who asked her, "Why don't more of your people [African Americans] come to these events?"

ENCOURAGING MUSICIANSHIP

An interest in music can be a wonderful source of enjoyment throughout life. Unblessed with musical ability myself, I can't teach my grandchildren a note or open professional doors for them. But any grandmother can do one thing that musical Lerotha and unmusical Sally both do—attend every one of your grandchildren's concerts that you can possibly go to—even if you have trouble spotting them on stage with the rest of the orchestra. This lets them know that their musical activities are valued. It also lets them know that *they* are valued. (I don't expect to follow Anna and her violin when she goes to Belgium next year with her high school orchestra, but I have made it to all her New Jersey school concerts—and of course, to the one at New York's Lincoln Center. And I plan to help her raise some of the money she'll need for that European trip.)

In our society, money talks—or sings—too. Offering a little is another way to show that you value musical activity. Some grandmothers pay for music lessons, or pay children for practicing, or for performances.

$-$ $$

Camp Grandma

Every summer, for a little over a week, most of Judy's ten grandchildren leave their parents at home while they come to "Camp Grandma" at Judy and Sam's lakeside cottage in Locust Grove, Virginia. The number of campers varies from year to year, with the two-year-olds still needing to stay at home and the teenagers likely to have jobs or other plans. Those who come do at least as much as they would do at any camp, and the added bonus is being with Grandma and each other. One of Judy's main motivations has been to give all her grandchildren time with their cousins, and she revels in the deep friendships that have developed.

Water sports include swimming, tubing, kayaking, and paddle-boating, all taught by waterfront coach Grandma, complete with whistle and safety rules: The younger ones all have to wear life jackets, and they all have to have a buddy to go in the water. Judy taught the children to fish, and how to clean and cook the fish.

Chores like cooking, table-setting, and cleaning up are shared with the help of a work chart, which, to Judy's surprise, turned out to be one of the children's favorite aspects of the week. Cooking is special fun on "Wacky Wednesdays," when the young cooks might make Green Eggs and Ham, Roast Beast, Hand Sandwiches (grilled cheese in hand shapes), or Kitty Litter Cake ("the cat's meow!").

And what camp would be complete without arts and crafts? Every year, Judy buys plain T-shirts, which she and the children decorate by hand with fabric paint, printing "Camp Grandma" and the year on the front and the children's names on the back. She also takes along at least one other project, which might, like a recent scrapbook activity, come in a kit from the crafts store near her home in Falls Church. Judy has also taught the three girls, ages eight to twelve, how to cut out patterns and to sew skirts and blouses, and both girls and boys how to knit.

RUNNING YOUR OWN GRANDKIDS' CAMP

Not all of us, of course, have lakeside cottages, not all of us have had Judy's experience teaching kindergarten, and not all of us would be up for hosting a bevy of children for a week at a time. But all of us can pick bits and pieces from the program at Camp Grandma and have special fun with one or more grandchildren. Whether you hold "camp" for one or a dozen, you'll be creating great memories that the children will carry into adulthood.

Inexpensive T-shirts are easy to come by, and if you don't have confidence in your or your grandchild's artistic ability, you can buy stencils at your neighborhood art or crafts store. Or you can tie-dye the T-shirts. Be sure to make one for yourself too, to wear at the gym—and you'll all have a wearable memory of your time together.

The crafts stores that have sprung up all over the country are treasure troves of ideas, where you're limited only by your imagination and the age levels of the children who will be taking part. Many kits provide how-to directions, and usually the salespeople are quite helpful in guiding you through the activities.

(They want you to keep coming back!) Some of Camp Grandma's evening activities can also be done by any grandparent: read aloud every night from a favorite book; play games like Clue, Monopoly, or bingo; and light sparklers outside to create more sparkling memories.

Make Your Own Stone

On a recent visit from her home in Kansas to her grandmother's home in Muncie, Indiana, Katie, age ten, made a one-foot (30.5-centimeter)-high head of a *grot* from *hypertufa*. What are these strange words? Grots are whimsical goblin-type creatures that, according to one New Zealand expert, "inhabit only dark forest floors and gloomy garden corners and are quite deficient in social skills." And hypertufa is a spongy, porous substance similar to limestone, made from cement, sand, peat moss, perlite (a lightweight volcanic glass), and water.

Since Katie and her family live 600 miles (966 kilometers) away from Grandma Emilie, visits are limited and time together precious. "We try to have activities planned and organized before their arrival to make the best use of our time," Emilie says. So she bought hypertufa supplies ahead of time at a local garden store and a building supply store, assembled them, and spent several hours time working with Katie. Emilie made a couple of planters, and Katie made her grot head. Because the head took time to dry, Emilie ended up taking it the 600 miles (966 kilometers) back to Kansas on her next visit to her son's family, and now it sits on their doorstep, welcoming visitors. Apparently, it's more sociable than the typical grot.

GREAT GROTS

"The hypertufa procedure is messy, but it's fun," says Emilie, who learned the how-to from a cultural center in Muncie, and then got guidance online. She prepared before her grandchildren's visit by assembling the materials: cement, perlite, peat moss, rubber gloves, a trowel, a wheelbarrow (you can also use a different large container), molds (like old containers and plastic gallon jugs), brushes, a water hose, a sturdy base larger than the molds, and a large sheet of heavy plastic to cover her patio to protect the surface.

The procedure is too complex to describe completely here, so if there is no class in your area (check with your local garden store), follow the instructions on one or more of some one thousand hypertufa websites. Emilie likes **www.efildoog-nz.com** and **www.backyardgardener.com**. Briefly, you mix the ingredients to a mud-pie consistency, form your shapes, let it set for 24 hours without moving it, shape and brush it, and then leave it to cure and set for at least a week. Iain Hay of the Copper Leaf garden store in Jordan Village, Ontario, suggests making leaf imprints while the mixture is wet. You can make tubs to use as planters, stepping stones, sculptures, and whatever else your imagination cooks up, including those shy grots.

Keys to Music

"My kids wouldn't practice when I tried to teach them, but my grandkids do!" says Sharon, whose twenty-four piano pupils in Wilmington, Delaware, include three of her five grandchildren. (The other two live in Washington State, too far away to come to Grandma's house for piano lessons.) "There's just something about skipping a generation."

Sharon had a strong precedent for taking on her grandchildren as music students. For several years, her own mother, also a piano teacher, lived in an apartment attached to Sharon's house, and after Sharon found that teaching her own children wasn't producing fruitful results, she would just send them through the door to their grandmother's music studio, where they did very well.

Now, she says that her own grandchildren, Mariah, age 16, Robert, 13½, and Julia, 10½, "don't give me a hard time at all." At one time, however, one (who shall be nameless), who started young was not practicing, and was "fired" by Grandma. A couple of years later, the grandkid/pupil came back to Grandma's studio and worked hard. All the grandchildren have made music an important part of their lives: Mariah also plays clarinet and bass recorder; Robert plays guitar, drums, and keyboard; and Julia, cello and French horn. Clearly, musical talent runs—even gallops—in this family!

"GRANDMA, TEACH ME!"

For all you musical grandmothers, it's hard to resist a plea like that, but Sharon urges that no matter how well you play piano or any other instrument, you take them on as pupils only if you know how to teach music. Sharon earned a bachelor's degree in music, studied teaching methods with her mother, and continues to learn about her profession, attending workshops and conferences for music teachers and continuing to read. She recommends the following books: *Teaching Piano Successfully,* by Jane and James Bastien, and *How to Teach Piano*, by Denis Agay. And she recommends the magazines: *Clavier* and its student magazine, *Piano Explore,* and *Keyboard Companion.* By joining the Music Teachers National Association, you get the magazine *American Music Teacher* and the opportunity to attend many teacher-training events and enter students in festivals.

Sharon's lessons include written theory ("like grammar if you're teaching English"), history of music, technical work like scales, and the actual musical pieces. She also has her pupils learn sight reading and ear training. "I like to make them into all-round musicians."

Every one of Sharon's pupils has an assignment book, and some of the youngsters ask to be graded at every lesson, or even on every piece. So Sharon sometimes uses a ten-point grading system, with ten being the best score, depending on how well prepared the student is and whether she or he has done what was supposed to be done. She has also written smiley faces into an assignment book when a piece was well done, with frowning faces for pieces that need a lot of work and sometimes a face that's half-smile, half-frown. And she urges the students to keep a practice record. So she writes down the days of the week, including lesson day, and asks the students to write down how many minutes they practiced before and after their lessons and every day in between. "This way, they can keep track of what they're doing—and so can I," she says.

On The Slopes with Nana

"Nana, I have a question for you," nine-year-old Jarred said. "Why were you so fast on our first days of skiing and then you got so slow you could hardly keep up?" "Jarred," laughed Leslie, "I didn't get any slower—you got faster!"

Leslie, Brent, and their twin daughters had skied for years, first on local slopes near their home in Madison, Wisconsin, and then going in their camper van to the bigger mountains in Colorado. So when their first grandchild came along, it was only natural to start Jarred on skis as soon as possible. "At age four," says Leslie, "he looked like a little penguin in his rented boots and skis!" Of course, the fact that Brent is a ski instructor made it easy to get Jarred started.

Last year, Leslie flew from Madison to her daughter's home in Connecticut, where she spent a couple of days with Jarred, his sister, and three brothers (two sets of twins), and then flew with Jarred to Colorado where he skied with Nana and Papa for five days. Jarred missed a few days of school, but Leslie, a former teacher, brought his homework along, and saw that he did it on the flights and every afternoon after skiing. Leslie flew with him back to Connecticut, and then she returned to Colorado for more skiing. "It was such a success that we are doing it again this year," says this frequent flier and skier. "Through skiing, we have been able to enjoy one-on-one time with Jarred," Leslie says, "and show him how much we love and care about him."

SAFETY AND SUCCESS ON THE SLOPES

At first, Jarred went down the "bunny hill" with his hands on his knees, while the rest of the family stood at the bottom of the hill, cheered him on, and caught him. Next, he progressed to the chair lift, and his family was able to control his speed by having him wear a harness and "leash" as a preschooler. He first skied on the bigger trails at age seven, still under expert guidance.

"We wanted Jarred to have fun, but to be able to ski under control," Leslie says. He uses short skis and has focused on learning how to turn so that he can keep to a safe speed, and he can now ski with Nana and Papa through all kinds of conditions. Although he wants to race with other kids, that will come later. Meanwhile, Leslie reminds him, "Jarred, wait up for us!"

"When grandkids are involved, a condo provides a relaxing, homey atmosphere," says Leslie. Many ski resorts are now catering more to families, which has led to the opening of reasonably priced condos and hotels near the slopes.

And for all the grannies who don't have a ski instructor in the family, there are many opportunities for children to learn how to ski safely and enjoyably. An excellent website, **www.mom steam.com**, has good advice (from Sue Bay, director of children's programs for The Aspen Skiing Company in Aspen, Colorado) and for parents (and grandparents) who want to enjoy skiing with children. There's also a blizzard of books about kids and skiing.

Tell Your Culture's Stories

L ike an increasing number of children today, Judith's four grandchildren, ages six to twelve, are the offspring of interfaith marriages. Aware that unions of partners of different religious or ethnic backgrounds often result in one parent's cultural legacy becoming lost to the children, Judith has taken upon herself the role of Jewish Grandmother.

"The narratives Jews have been telling for thousands of years are part of my grandchildren's heritage," she says. "Every culture has its stories, and I am doing my best to be sure they know the ones some of their ancestors have told."

And so Judith tells stories. At holiday celebrations, and also through email and postal mail, Judith shares the long-running serial she has written, called "*Granny Judy's Tales of Jewish Holidays.*" Her account of the Jewish New Year, for example, explains why in 2009 Jews celebrate the year 5770, because Jewish tradition says that God finished creating the world 5770 years ago. She explains holiday rituals like eating apples and honey (to assure a sweet year ahead) and casting bread crumbs into running water (to symbolically get rid of last year's regrets and make a fresh start in the year just beginning).

Judith also hosts her sons, her Christian daughters-in-law, and her grandchildren for holiday parties and dinners, at which she serves traditional foods. The children help with the cooking and table setting.

THE SUCCESSFUL STORYTELLER

A major reason for her family's embrace of Granny Judy's tales is that Judith is exquisitely sensitive to the feelings of her daughters-in-law. She does not contradict the Christian narratives her grandchildren have learned at Sunday school and from their mothers; she simply adds another layer of meaning. As a result, the children's mothers are staunch supporters of Judith's contributions.

She encourages other grandmothers who want to be their families' bearers of tradition to read as widely as they can in the traditions and texts of their religion or their ethnic culture and to make their accounts as faithful as possible to these sources. "Be honest," she says. "Don't sugar-coat the distressing stuff, like the Biblical plagues, especially the one about the death of the first born, or like unpleasant historical episodes in the country of your ancestors." Also, it's important to keep an open mind, to acknowledge the stories of other cultures, to encourage the children to ask questions, and to answer them as honestly as possible. And it's okay to say, "I don't know, but I'll try to find out."

Grandparents can also find help in a 2007 book *Twenty Things for Grandparents of Interfaith Children to Do,* by Rabbi Kerry M. Olitzky and Paul Golin, and through a 2008 program, The Grandparents Circle, launched by the Jewish Outreach Institute (JOI) especially for grandparents of interfaith children. To learn about the program or find out how to start one in your area, email Liz Marcovitz at lmarcovitz@joi.org.

$-$$

Help Your Grandchildren to Give

During Diwali, the Hindu festival of lights, which falls in early November, nine-year-old Akash's grandmother encourages his efforts to raise money in Brooklyn to send to impoverished children in Afghanistan. In Chicago, Mary instills the meaning of Kwanzaa in her grandchildren, encouraging them to live their lives with purpose and responsibility. In Quincy, Illinois, one pair of grandparents who remain anonymous include in their Christmas celebrations a trip with their three grandchildren to a supermarket where they pay the grocery bills for struggling families. And in another Illinois community, Marianne's eight grandchildren receive, as one of their eight Hanukkah gifts, a bookmark telling the child that a book was purchased in his or her name and given to a needy youngster in Israel.

When I asked my own grandchildren this past holiday season what kinds of charitable gifts they would like me to make in their names, they came up with a variety of causes: a children's hospital, a health center that helps adolescents, a service that rescues downed pilots or lost hikers, and a wildlife fund that saves endangered animals. I researched organizations, checked back with the children for their approval, and then made the contributions, giving their names and addresses so that they will be informed of the work the groups do. I'll be interested to see whether they will continue their interest in these causes from year to year or whether they will want to fund different ones. Meanwhile, they enjoy knowing that one of their holiday gifts is giving to others, and I hope they'll continue to enjoy giving when the money will be coming out of their own pockets!

ENCOURAGING GENEROSITY

Children can learn all year round that giving can sometimes be even better than receiving. Carol Weisman, a grandmother and the author of *Raising Charitable Children,* suggests asking a child on his or her birthday questions like, "How would you like to change the world in the next year? What made you happy or sad during the past year? What would you like to do for someone else?" Carol says, "You can have some really meaningful conversations that can lead to bettering other people's lives, as well as making an important impact on the child's own life."

For example, after ten-year-old Carrie said, "I would like to stop bullying," her grandparents brought an anti-bullying program to Carrie's school. A four-year-old boy who confessed after seeing TV reports about Hurricane Katrina that he was afraid of water and had been wetting his bed made a donation to victims of flooding. That was the last time he wet the bed.

Other suggestions from Carol:

- For a nearby agency, phone ahead, speak to a development person, and take your grandchild there in person.
- Give your grandchild a scrapbook where she or he can put drawings, photos, and other records of whatever the child does that helps others.

- Hold a family philanthropy meeting where several grandchildren can get together and decide what they want to support.
- Helpful books include *A Kid's Guide to Giving*, by Freddi Zeiler and Ward Schumaker, and *The Kids Guide to Service Projects: Over 500 Service Ideas for Young People Who Want to Make a Difference*, by Barbara A. Lewis and Pamela Espeland.

$ $$

Plan a Perfect Day

*N*ot all planned outings with children go as smoothly as you had hoped, but one of mine with seven-year-old Nina could not have been more perfect. Since we live fairly close to American Girl Place in New York (**www.american girl.com**), a mega-store that sells dolls and doll clothes and doll accessories like beds and horses and pet dogs and books and all kinds of other related items that you can drop a small fortune on, along with a restaurant and theater, I splurged on an American Girl day for just the two of us, Nina and me.

After Opa [German word for grandfather] and I gave Nina her longed-for doll, he left with Nina's mother and big sister, and Nina and I rode the escalator up to the café. Little seats are provided so that dolls can join their owners at the table, and if a girl does not have (or forgot) her own doll, she can borrow one for the mealtime. Napkins are held by hair scrunchies with a white-and-yellow daisy (to keep), every table holds a little box with slips of paper with conversation-encouraging questions and tiny mugs are set at the doll's place. Lunch servings ($24 prix fixe plus tax at this writing includes appetizers, main course, dessert, and drinks) gave us more food than either of us could finish, and when the server found out that Nina was celebrating her birthday, he lit a candle on her cupcake, asked her name, and sang "Happy Birthday." As an added after-bonus, Nina's enjoyment of the cinnamon buns served with lunch led to my promise that the next time she visited me, we would make our own. And we did, following my mother's (Nina's great-grandmother's) recipe, which my youngest daughter, Dorri, had written up for the delightful book of essays and recipes, *At Grandmother's Table: Women Write about Food, Life and the Enduring Bond between Grandmothers and Granddaughters,* edited by Ellen Berkeley.

After lunch, we went into the theater where we watched *Circle of Friends,* a musical featuring a dozen talented girls and three adults, telling the stories of the historical dolls, woven into a story about friendship—how it feels when you think your best friend doesn't like you any more, and what to do with your feelings. The best part of the day for me was seeing Nina's day-long smile!

PLANNING YOUR OWN DAY

Grannies seem to agree unanimously that the best days with grandchildren are one-on-one affairs: one grandmother, one grandchild. No siblings. No parents. No friends. Not even the grandfather, just the two of you.

And don't make it a surprise. I am no longer a fan of surprises. Over the course of many years, I have given and received surprise parties for various occasions. When I was the recipient, it was always such a drag having to pretend I was surprised. And when I was the giver, it was just as much of a drag doing all the cloak-and-dagger planning so that the guest wouldn't know what was up. And then wondering: Was he really surprised? So a few years ago, our family decided that surprise parties were history. The problem with doing a special day with a grandchild as a surprise means that the child can't have the fun of antici-pation, which is often half the excitement—thinking about it, dreaming about it. Of course, with a young child, you don't want to tell her about the event too soon, or she's likely to ask her parents (or you) upward of twenty times a day, with slight variations: "When am I going out with Oma?" "Is it tomorrow?" "Next week?" "When?"

What has worked for me has been to ask my grandchildren what they want to do—or to propose an outing and ask them what they think of it. Sometimes the feedback to that squelched a brilliant idea of mine forever. But at other times, my grandchildren's enthusiasm has made all the effort of planning—and the cost of paying for it—worthwhile, like the time I took nine-year-old Lisa to see *The Lion King* on Broadway. She had seen the movie, she knew the songs, the older grandchildren had seen it when she was too young to go, and by now she was eager to experience it for herself. I was just as eager to have that special day with her. Perfection!

Travel with a Grandchild

When Dee told her friends she was taking her seven-year-old granddaughter, Michaela, to London for a week, reactions ranged from "Oh, what fun!" to "She's too young." The first reaction turned out to be the right one, since Dee found Michaela to be a wonderful traveling companion.

It helped that Dee, whom Michaela calls Mimi, had been to London several times and knew the lay of the land. It also helped that she put a lot of time, thought, and effort into preparing for the journey. Her first move was to post a question in the "Person to Person" section of the magazine *International Travel News* (**www.intltravelnews.com**), asking for advice on traveling with a young child. Her next step was contacting a family law attorney, who advised her about getting necessary documents.

"The trip opened Michaela's eyes to a world wider than she ever knew existed, and it will, I hope, be the first of many such trips for her," says Dee. Michaela learned many tools of successful travel. She helped to plan the trip by reading the children's map that Dee had bought on a previous London stay, using the stickers that came with it to mark the attractions they visited. Michaela learned to read the Underground maps to figure out their routes, as well. She also honed her photography skills, often grabbing Mimi's camera to snap her own unique perspective of London sights. Back home, Dee uploaded their photos to an online site (**www.shutterfly.com**) and helped Michaela create her own book.

Dee learned too. "The most valuable lesson I learned was to slow down and enjoy the moment, a lesson Michaela taught me on our last day in London." As they were sitting by the Thames enjoying ice-cream cones, Dee asked where Michaela wanted to go next. "Right now," Michaela replied, "I just want to eat my ice cream."

TIPS FOR TRAVELING WITH A YOUNG CHILD

Involving Michaela in planning for their trip was a major element in its success. Dee and Michaela read books about visiting London with a child to help them draw up a list of "must-sees." If you're going to a place that doesn't have books about it, look for information on the Internet or contact the area's tourism office or chamber of commerce, which are available on the web or by phone.

Staying at an apartment instead of a hotel is another good idea. When I went to Berlin with my daughter and grandchildren, we did the same things Dee did: bought breakfast, snacks, and drinks in the supermarket and ate breakfast in the apartment. A couple of evenings, we ate dinner in from take-out restaurants. A flat is a welcome oasis for tired children and grannies.

The American Society of Travel Agents (**www.asta.org**) recommends doing a test run before planning a big trip: taking a day or overnight trip to see how being alone with your grandchild without the parents will work. From babyhood, Michaela had spent overnights with Mimi, and from age three, they had taken weekend trips, including annual sojourns to their church's "Grandcamp." ASTA recommends taking only one child, or at most two, at a time. And it stresses the need to have the child's identification documents, health insurance information, medical history, contact information, recent photos, and notarized permission from both parents.

You can get help from a travel agent who specializes in intergenerational travel. Or you might be more comfortable taking your grandchild on a group experience. Some travel agents specialize in "grand travel," and a number of companies run group trips. Elderhostel intergenerational programs (**www. elderhostel.org/programs**), for example, offer a wide range of domestic and international experiences.

Enter a Fantasy World

Walking into twelve-year-old Sara's bedroom in East Casper, Wyoming, you enter another world, one filled with fairies and unicorns, dolphins and mermaids, castles and hills. Where did this world come from? When Sara was six, her grandmother, Betsy, looked at Sara's room and saw four bare walls. Sara, who had been living with her grandparents since infancy, never complained about her room, but Betsy decided she wanted to do something.

For years, Betsy had encouraged Sara's love of fairy tales, fantasy, and myth, by giving her books, including those she had loved as a child, like *Peter Pan,* and telling her stories. With this in mind, Betsy asked her friend, Tisa Bilek, an interior painter nearby in Casper, what Tisa could paint in Sara's room. "We can do anything Sara wants," Tisa said. So Tisa and Sara sat cross-legged on the floor of Sara's room and brainstormed, as Sara came up with her ideas, and Tisa thought about how to implement them.

The result is a magical kingdom. As you go into the room, you come upon a breakaway castle, feeling as if you are inside the castle looking out, where you see hills, another castle, a bluebird, and a unicorn looking back at you. On another wall, you see a mermaid sitting on top of rocks and a dolphin jumping out of the ocean. A locked door leads outside to a lush garden where an angel stands guard. And the painted clouds on the ceiling make you feel as if you're standing outdoors.

Six years later, Sara still loves welcoming friends to her fantasy room. Her cousins—Betsy's nine other grandchildren, who range in age from 10 months to 19 years—also love to enter this world.

CREATING ANOTHER WORLD

Whether your grandchild's special passion is fairies or horses and cowboys, Betsy urges other grandmothers to think about making a child's room very special.

Of course, for a grandchild not living with you, you need to consult the child's parents to see if this fits in with their decorating plans. Then you can either do the painting yourself or find a professional to do the work. If you don't know of anyone, type "residential muralist" or "faux finisher" into your search engine, along with the name of your city, and you are likely to come up with an artist who can make your—and your grandchild's— dream room come to life. Some artists maintain websites showing other work they have done, which will help you choose.

According to Kathleen Spicer, a New York artist who does this kind of work, "speaking on the phone with an artist is almost useless." To really make your grandchild's dream come true, the artist will need to see the child's home, general décor, and the colors of the furniture in the room. And you and your grandchild will need to talk with the artist about what you have in mind. For your part, you will want to see the artist's portfolio of other rooms that she or he has painted, and you will want to get the names of a couple of people who can provide references. Then you will need to work out a time frame and agree on the price. And then you're all set to enter the room of a child's dreams.

Creativity across Generations

When Ke-Sook Lee was in grade school in Seoul, South Korea, and sharing a room with her grandmother, she learned sewing "as if it were a necessity of life and as important as writing or reading." Sewing was indeed a necessity, since the children's cotton socks wore out quickly, and the women of the house gathered in the evenings to mend them. Ke-Sook especially enjoyed watching her grandmother as she patiently made clothes for Ke-Sook's doll and embroidered red flowers on those little socks, and the endurance and creativity the older woman displayed bore fruit in her granddaughter's adult years.

As a homemaker living in the United States, Ke-Sook embroidered, crocheted, sewed her own dresses, and made quilts and blankets. Then, as the holder of two Bachelor of Fine Arts degrees, she integrated stitching into her artwork. Today, an artist in Kansas City, Missouri, she exhibits her creative and contemporary stitchery in prestigious museums around the country. One installation of hand-embroidered vintage handkerchiefs, titled *One Hundred Faceless Women,* pays tribute to her grandmother's use of embroidery to express her emotions (since, like many Korean women of that time, she could neither read nor write) and reflects Ke-Sook's identity and experiences from her own life. To learn more about Ke-Sook's art, go to **www.ke-sooklee.com** or www.georgebillis.com/artists/ke-sook_lee.html.

ANOTHER GRANDMOTHER'S INSPIRATION

Robin O'Brien of Winchester, England, is another grand-daughter inspired by her grandmother's fine needlework. Robin was only eight years old when her grandmother taught her the basic chain stitch. "During that summer, I crocheted a chain that went around the entire outside of my house two times!" she says. She subsequently learned knitting, cross-stitching, quilt-making, and rug-hooking. And today some of her most intimate family times occur when she and her mother knit together. "For the most part," Robin says, "we sit there in silence, though we are somehow connected, like two balls of wool. Just as I felt I had a special bond with my grandmother through knitting, I feel I have a stronger bond with my mother because of our love of it." This craft learned at her grandmother's knee has contributed to the emotional richness of Robin's life, which she often writes about on her website, **www.selfimprovementtechniques.com**.

Once more, we see how a grandmother's example and a shared activity can lead to unforeseen, often inspired results. For tips about helping your grandchildren learn to crochet, go to **http://kniting.thecrochettips.com/index.php/59/crochet-for-beginners/**.

Classmates: Nana and Me

Mary had been out of college for forty years, and her grandson Nate, age eight, would not matriculate for another ten. But last summer, Mary and Nate were roommates at Michigan State University, one of a growing number of colleges sponsoring intergenerational programs. MSU's Grandparents University in East Lansing offers grandparents (who don't have to be alumni) and grandchildren (ages eight to twelve) the chance to spend three days taking three different classes. Classes might include horses, archery, forensic entomology, digital photo editing, virtual maps, and some 100 other offerings from fourteen different university departments. Tuition runs about $500, and some scholarships are available.

Before classes began, Nate, who had brought his bike, and Mary, who rented one, cycled over to a "Tour of the World," where they entered a large room divided into stations staffed by people from Colombia, Korea, Japan, Mali, Saudi Arabia, and other nations. Nate learned how to sing in Spanish, write his name in Chinese, and do Thai boxing. Nana served as Nate's photographer and tour guide, seeing that he got from one station to the next.

The team made it into Nate's first choice, the popular Lego Robotics, where they found a partly built robot, a box of tiny parts, and an instruction manual. Mary drew upon her childhood "Tinker Toy" experience to help Nate put it together, and he programmed it to carry out commands (mainly "Go here," "Go there," and "Turn around"), "a good mix of our combined skills." For the class "Where does milk come from?" they went to the university's dairy farm, where Nate put his hand in a cow's belly during a demonstration of a veterinary research project. Their last class, "Treasure Hunting," gave each child a portable Global Positioning System. The children ran all over campus with their GPS units following hidden clues, with winded grandparents bringing up the rear.

Mary's favorite part was the quality time she and Nate spent together learning, exploring, and discovering new ways to challenge and inspire their imaginations. Nate's favorite part: whichever activity he had done most recently! At the time he was doing them, every class was his favorite.

COOL COEDS

Since some classes fill up quickly, every family is asked to select ten classes, with assignments made on a first-come, first-serve basis. Mary went online (**www.grandparents.msu.edu**) as soon as enrollment opened in December for the next summer, printed out the classes, and worked with Nate to select and prioritize his choices. All pre-event registration is done by email. (Remember when people asked if you had email? Now they ask, "What's your email address?") Nate and Nana left their home in Glenview, Illinois, a day early so that they could spend the night at a campus hotel and check in at their dorm early the next morning to have maximum time for activities.

Planning ahead helps you to get the "early bird" rate for tuition and to have the best chance of getting your first choice of classes. If you don't want to take or rent bicycles, you can take shuttle buses between activities. Information packets from MSU include maps of the campus, packing suggestions, and descriptions of evening activities, like swimming, skating, movies, and going to the museum.

Go to Grandparents' Day

When I was invited to visit Anna's third-grade class for Grandparents' Day (decreed by President Jimmy Carter as the first Sunday after Labor Day) to talk about what life was like when I was their age, I jumped at the chance. In the classroom, I wrote the following list on the blackboard:

1. WHAT WE DIDN'T HAVE WHEN I WAS EIGHT YEARS OLD: Computers, email, VCRs, DVDs, CDs, sweetened breakfast cereals, microwave ovens, in-line skates, snow-blowers, running shoes, digital watches, felt-tip markers, push-button phones, cell phones, answering machines, mountain bikes, helmets for bike-riding, and seat belts in cars.

2. WHAT WE DID HAVE: Paper dolls, jump ropes, milk in glass bottles delivered to our home, deliveries of big blocks of ice to our home, roller skates with skate keys that you wore on a string around your neck, jacks, pickup sticks, radio programs just for kids (*Let's Pretend* on Saturday mornings), trolley cars, and Super Hero comic books. (I had not thought about some of these things for years, and it was fun, albeit sobering, catching up with my old memories, which seemed to come from an ancient era.)

PREPARING FOR GRANDPARENTS' DAY

If your grandchild's school does not have a Grandparents' Day in its schedule, ask your grandchild's parent to ask the teacher if she or he would be interested in having you come to speak to the children, either on the above topics or about your work, volunteer activities, travels, or any other topic appropriate for the age group.

Kids love even the smallest presents, so you might take inexpensive handouts for all the children. Possibilities include a pencil with a cute pattern or a Post-it pad in a die-cut design or fluorescent color. No food, since there's too much danger of running into an allergy.

You can also create a handout. Make an interactive form by asking questions and leaving blanks for the kids to fill in. Have a Q&A at the end of your visit, and ask the kids to read their answers. Or give them questions that they can use to interview their parents or other adults. Ask the teacher if she or he would like to schedule a follow-up discussion based on the answers. These are possible interview questions: What type of work do you do? Have you ever done any volunteer work? What are some exciting places you have visited? What did you like about them?

You have interesting experiences and memories that you may not have thought of sharing with your grandchildren and their friends. A neighbor of mine wrote a bestselling memoir as the result of his grandchildren's questions about his past.

When you go, remember that kids embarrass easily, so look as normal (translation: unobtrusive) as possible. Forget the crazy hairdo, leave your old-lady oxfords, ankle-high sneakers, and six-inch heels in your closet, and dress as if you didn't want people in the street to turn around and stare at you.

Elderhostelers and Grandkids

Kelsie Lee's trip to Costa Rica was the first of several journeys she took with Granny Shirley Bee, known to Kelsie Lee as "Mommy Bee." "I chose that one first, of all the Elderhostel intergenerational trips," says Shirley Bee, "because I am a bit of a nature freak and I wanted to share my interest in bugs, birds, butterflies, trees, and plants with Kelsie Lee." The six children on the trip bonded quickly, leaving a little time for adults to get together, as well. Although ten-year-old Kelsie Lee enjoyed many aspects of the nature program, the highlight for her may have been the evening when a few local young people taught everyone to dance the salsa and a handsome boy asked her to dance.

With the knowledge and appreciation for the environment that Kelsie Lee gained on that first trip, she eagerly went with Mommy Bee the following year to the Galapagos, which was another nature bonanza. "What I loved the best—besides being with my grandmother—was swimming with sea lions, the way they came right up to your face!" She also liked the snorkeling and standing very close to a blue-footed booby (a tropical seabird). She and Mommy Bee hiked and visited islands with exotic birds and animals. The last trip the duo took together was to the Grand Canyon, where they stayed at a hotel owned by Native Americans and had a thrilling helicopter ride out of the canyon.

Shirley Bee chose Elderhostel's intergenerational trips because she had found on previous Elderhostel trips people who "were wonderful folks, intelligent, friendly, interesting, and interested in learning. They added a great deal to the trips." Kelsie Lee also appreciated being able to meet new people and see new places.

MAKING IT WORK

Elderhostel, as its name implies, is known for its educational, moderately priced programs for older people in many U.S. and international locations. This popular institution also offers about 300 vacations designed specifically for grandparents and grand-children. They include adventure trips with rock-climbing, kayaking, and hiking; historical and cultural experiences; and many other trips, focusing on the circus, baseball, art, animals, and a host of other interests. To search for programs by age range (the grandchildren's, not yours!), dates, locations, and other criteria, go to: **www.elderhostel.org/programs/search_res.asp?key word=intergenerational+trips**.

Although many programs have group leaders who work with the children, as well as the adults, you remain the primary supervisor of your grandchild or grandchildren. Some programs limit participants to no more than one child per adult, while others will allow you to bring as many as four grandchildren. The organization always sends a booklet that describes each day's activities; suggests clothing and other items to bring, reading materials, and any immunization shots you might need; and provides a list of the participants, as well as addresses and phone numbers of the hotels where you will be staying (for your family or anyone needing to contact you).

Many travel companies offer intergenerational programs. To find a tour, type "intergenerational travel" into your search engine. Then evaluate tours according to criteria suggested by Tom Easthope, the head of a Washington-based agency (**www.generationstouringcompany.com**) that offers small-group travel experiences: Does the trip offer both fun and education, does it respect cultures and the environment, will you have time to bond as a family, does it provide good value, and are your prepayments protected by an insurance plan?

Adolescence (Ages 12 to 18)

That little girl who used to bound onto your lap and smother you with kisses and the little boy who would run up to you with bear hugs now have other outlets for their affection (even if only in their minds). Adolescents these days have a lot on their plates, between the demands of school, extracurricular activities, and social life. Then there are their MP3s and their cell phones and other vital accoutrements of modern adolescent life. Their days are busy, and sometimes it feels as if they don't have time for you. They do have less time and less inclination to talk to anyone they didn't "friend" in Facebook.

But there will always be a place somewhere in their lives for a loving, interested, supportive grandmother. Especially if you fit in with the activities that are important to them, like taking your 12-year-old granddaughter shopping for her first bra or bravely sitting in the "death seat" while your 16-year-old grandson practices his driving—and if you bite your tongue before saying anything trying to make them feel guilty for not calling or visiting the way they did when they were six!

Your role is different now. You can be the recipient of confidences that a teenager might not want to share with a parent. You can be a fount of wisdom and a teller of tales about when their parents were young, as long as you keep your stories lively (preferably full of parental misdeeds) and minus moralizing. You can have abstract and far-ranging conversations that were not possible in earlier years. And you can sometimes offer special opportunities that parents cannot, such as exotic travel, pricey concerts and shows, and chances to do things out of the ordinary. You can also provide valuable one-on-one time when you can experience and talk about shared interests and show your interest in those activities that you don't share.

The role of grandmother to a preteen and teenager is still precious and unique. And as you'll see in the following pages, you still have many opportunities and many avenues to play a special role in their lives.

$-$$

Take a Grandchild to Breakfast

Marge, an artist in Evanston, Illinois, is lucky enough to live near nine of her fourteen grandchildren. One way she sees them regularly is to take them out, one at a time, to breakfast before school, a practice she started when the children were in fourth grade and has continued through the high school years. "Although a few of the kids like to sleep in," Marge says, "for most of them, this time before school seems to work best."

Marge picks up the grandchild of the day at 6:30, keeps close watch over the time ("I never want to be responsible for anyone's coming to school late!"), and then takes him or her directly to school. Over pancakes, she learns about the children's lives, interests, questions, and problems. Often the conversation begins when the child asks, "Grandma, what do you think about . . ." some item in the news. At age sixteen Jacob, who planned to seek an ROTC scholarship in college, often talked about the war in Iraq. Ellen, thirteen, whose interest in fashion, clothes, and dressmaking far exceeded her grandmother's, would tell Marge about the latest styles. Marge, an avid reader, often asks the children about the books they are reading in school. When Andrew, twelve, talked about the book, *There Are No Children Here,* by Alex Kotlowitz, about growing up in subsidized housing projects, this led to a conversation about the differences between the lives of the children in the book and his own life in a prosperous suburb.

The success of these "power breakfasts" can be seen in the fact that the grandchildren often call Marge to remind her that it's pancake time again, and stay super-vigilant about whose turn it is to go next. These early get-togethers are manageable for both generations in terms of time and are fairly inexpensive.

TIPS FOR SUCCESSFUL BREAKFASTING

First, you need to establish that the grandchild you want to take out is ready to communicate early in the morning. Some children take longer to wake up, and if they see getting up early as a chore, you won't accomplish your goal of a special one-on-one connection. For these children, it will be better to plan for lunch or dinner on a day they don't have school.

Find a breakfast spot that's close enough to school so that you won't have to worry about running into traffic and making the child late. It also should be one either that the child herself has chosen, or that you are pretty sure will have enough offerings to please the palate, especially if the child is a finicky eater.

Of course, you also need to be sure that the arrangement is okay with the parents, who may feel pressured to get up early themselves!

Then, as Marge says, "You have to kind of 'read' the kids. I try to steer the conversation to something they know more about than I do. I ask lots of questions."

Fortunately, you're the granny and not the parent, so you don't have to monitor the child's food choices! This is not the time to impose a diet, to say, "That's too fattening" or "Wouldn't you rather have this?" and the like. This is a fun time for both of you. Keep it that way!

Text-Message
Your Grandchild

used to telephone my thirteen-year-old granddaughter Anna on those afternoons when she didn't have an after-school activity or a get-together with a friend. She would come home from school at about 3:30, whereas her mother would not arrive home from work until about six. Anna usually used this time alone to do homework, practice her violin, grab a snack, read, watch TV, and who-knows-what-else. If I didn't live a two-hour-drive away, I would pop in from time to time, but instead, remembering my own adolescent love of the telephone (one attitude that does not seem to have changed over the generations), I often phoned her in the late afternoon.

However, adolescence is different now, and so is communication. Forty-two percent of 13- to 17-year-old cell phone users "text" daily. Since Anna got her new cell phone with text-messaging, her fingers are always busy, and she's always ready to send or receive text messages. She taught me how to create, send, and receive, and now this is our best time to "talk" about each other's doings (mostly hers!), as I learn about the museums she went to on her class trip to Boston, what she wore to her eighth-grade dinner dance, what books she's reading (recently Hemingway's *Old Man and the Sea*), what movies she wants to see, and what we should do the next time we have an in-person

visit, at her home or at ours. I do have to say that while her fingers fly so fast on her cell phone that her mother said, "I expect her to start a fire from friction alone!" I am much, much slower, so I keep my messages short, and I often follow up with the old-fashioned telephone call.

HOW 2 SPK TXT

Most cell phones are equipped to send text messages (also known as SMS, for Short Messaging Service), but for specific information on your own phone, you need to contact your mobile provider. Some plans include fees for text messages in your overall service, whereas others charge a fee for every message. (Mine charges 20 cents a message, either sent or received, and since I don't text that often, it's cheaper than the five dollars I would have to pay for unlimited texting.)

Your grandchild would probably be happy to show you how to text, but if she or he does not live nearby, it might be simpler to ask a technical support person at the toll-free number for your service provider. Since my service is provided by Verizon, I went to a nearby Verizon store and received help from a very patient young worker, who probably considered me a dinosaur, but one worthy to bring into the twenty-first century.

The basics are easy. You'll soon learn to use abbreviations (like *c u* for "see you," *wbs* for "write back soon," and *b4n* for "bye for now"), punctuation marks, and other symbols. You'll increase your speed too, but don't expect to be as fast as your grandchildren; they come equipped with flying fingers! If you want to be really hip when texting teenagers, use popular abbreviations, which you can find by googling "teen abbreviations" or "teen lingo." Two useful sites are **www.teenchat decoder.com/parental-lookup/teenchat-a.html** and **www.net lingo.com/emailsh.cfm**. For more websites, check the Resources appendix toward the end of the book.

Blog with Your Family

W hen Annette and Harry set out for an exciting overseas vacation, they kept in touch with their five grandchildren by setting up a weblog, or blog. They took their laptop computer with them and every day transferred digital photos to the computer and added notes and comments about the places they had been, the things they did, and the people they met, with special attention to information the children would find interesting. For example, since they knew what sports fans their grandsons were, they sent photos and descriptions about the *haka,* or war dance, that they had seen performed in New Zealand, the same dance the New Zealand rugby team does before each match in an effort to intimidate their opponents in the same way the ancient Maori warriors did with hostile tribes.

A weblog doesn't have to be about exotic trips. It can be a family newsletter, sent out from home on a regular basis just to stay in touch. You, your children, and your grandchildren can regularly send photos of each other, jokes, poems, copies of school reports, and brief comments about what everyone is doing. And everyone who receives the blog can post a comment to everyone else.

HOW TO CREATE A BLOG

You can get free help in creating a blog. One of the most popular websites to go to for this is **www.blogger.com**, operated by the Internet company Google. Here, you find step-by-step instructions that walk you through the process. Basically, you do the following:

- Create an account on **www.google.com**.
- Come up with a name for your blog, for example, "Super Granny." You can change this later.
- Give your blog a URL (Internet address), for example, **http://OmaSally.blogspot.com**.
- Choose your template, or page design, for your blog. You can change this later.
- Create your personal profile. Here, you can tell whatever you want about yourself: your favorite activities, books, music, the names of all your family members (especially the grandchildren), and whatever else you want to tell your readers.
- Post one or more photos of yourself, your activities, family members, or anything else you want to show.
- Write a post. When you are happy with what you have written, click on "Publish."
- Your grandchildren and anyone else can now answer your postings, and you can have an ongoing dialog.
- Be careful not to include addresses or phone numbers.

Take a City Tour on a Segway

"I didn't realize at first that the applause was for me," said Wini, "until I looked over and saw this group of Parisians smiling and clapping; they had obviously seen my gray hair peeping out of my helmet and wanted to cheer me on!" Wini and Ben, her thirteen-year-old grandson, were among a small group taking a Segway tour in the heart of Paris. The Segway Human Transporter is a high-tech electric scooter that you ride on by standing on a platform between two big wheels. To make it go, you turn a control on its waist-high handlebars; to stop, you lean back; and to steer, you twist the left handlebar up or down. Speed can be locked at a minimum of 6.5 miles (10.5 kilometers) per hour; the maximum is 12.5 miles (20 kilometers) per hour.

Wini made their tour reservation with City Segway Tours in advance of this celebratory trip (in honor of Ben's Bar Mitzvah), and then after arrival in Paris, Wini and Ben went for a 30-minute orientation and practice session, before setting out on the streets with their guide. "At first, the Segway looked intimidating, as if it would be hard to balance," Wini says, "but it turned out to be easy because of the gyroscope technology." She found it a little scary crossing streets, even though the guide often went into the middle of an intersection to stop traffic, but Ben got the hang of it right away, and as soon as he was permitted to, he upped his speed so that he could whip around

corners and race along the streets and paths they covered as they went by the Eiffel Tower, the Louvre, and other landmarks they would visit (on foot) later in their stay. Wini's verdict: "It was an exhilarating experience for both of us." Ben's: "It was my favorite thing in Paris!"

PLAN YOUR SEGWAY TOUR

These tours are given in many U.S. and international cities, including Washington, D.C., Chicago, Atlanta, Vienna, Budapest, and others. For information and to make arrangements, go online to **www.citysegwaytours.com** or go to **www.google.com** and search for Segway tours.

- All the tour companies stipulate a minimum age, generally between ages 12 and 16.
- Reservations are required. You can make them online, by phone, or fax. (For Paris, call toll-free from North America (866-614-6218) or fax toll-free (206-984-2707.)
- Prices vary, from about $70 per person for a three-hour tour in a U.S. city to about $100 per person for a four- to five-hour tour in a foreign city.
- Everyone has to sign a waiver. There have not been any serious injuries, but people do fall off (that's why everyone wears a helmet!).
- To negotiate traffic and to see the best places, you're better off taking a guided tour, even though in some places you can rent the Segways and go on your own.

A Mission of Compassion

When Betsy heard through a church in Casper, Wyoming, that a group of adults and children could go on a mission sponsored by Horizon International to work with AIDS orphans in South Africa, she asked twelve-year-old Sara if she wanted to go. Sara eagerly said yes, and she and Betsy were among a group of thirty adults and children (ages eight to early twenties) from several denominations who spent two weeks in Cape Town and Limpopo Province.

The American children and adults put down a cement floor for a drop-in center for orphans, planted vegetable gardens for orphan-headed households, and made hospice visits. They also had fun through craft activities and outdoor games. Gunny-sack races were the most popular with the African children, who had never seen them before. And the groups connected through music, with the American and African children singing and dancing for each other, and through worship.

The visitors took some time out for sightseeing: in Kruger National Park, where they saw elephants (who started to charge their car); at the Boulders near Cape Town, where they got close to penguins, and bought African craft items; and at Table Mountain National Park, where they saw whales.

Some people might think that this kind of trip would be too intense for young children who have never experienced the kinds of privations the African orphans had, but Sara loved it, even though she told her grandmother how sad it was to see children who had lost their parents. Says Betsy, "It was a life-changing experience for all of us. Our American children came home with a new appreciation for all that we have." Sara said, "I'll never complain about silly things again."

MAKING THE MISSION WORK

Before signing up, Betsy's first concern was for safety. She knew that Horizon International (**www.horizoninternationalinc.com**) was a responsible organization, but still she checked references and talked with others who had gone to the same areas they would visit. Reassured, she and Sara began to make their preparations. For months, they discussed the history and culture of the people they would be visiting, including local food and water. They talked about the 17-hour flight and what to bring on the plane. After checking with their health department, Betsy and Sara got necessary shots and malaria prevention pills.

The journals that both Betsy and Sara kept during the trip helped them capture their memories of what they did, whom they saw, and how they felt. (In my own travels, I have learned, often to my dismay, that experiences I think I'll remember forever tend to fade away if I haven't written them down right away.)

To be ready for a trip like this, a child needs to be mature and responsible and to be able to follow directions easily. She or he should be respectful of other cultures and willing to learn from them. Sara has told her friends at home about her amazement at nine-year-olds who have to head a household and about the resourcefulness of children who can take scraps like wire and tin cans and make them into toy cars.

You and Your Grandkids on Video

After a visit to the Museum of Natural History, Maika's videos of live lizards helped us all to continue to enjoy the exhibit. She didn't have any elaborate equipment—just her digital camera (not all digitals take videos as well as stills). Maika downloaded the videos to my computer, so every time I have a burning need to see a gecko in action, I can just click on it and remember that visit. So can the other grandkids, who received the videos by email.

We haven't posted the lizards online, on one of the many free video hosting sites (listed in the Resources), but we could. It's easy and free, and a great way to share your videos. I did post one video on YouTube, which Anna, age fifteen, took with her grandfather's digital camera. Next time, we'll do the grandkids' activities, like the video Nancy shot of Anna and Nina singing Opa a happy birthday concert, which she then put on a disk that we can play in our DVD player.

YOUR YOUTUBE DEBUT

To set up your video studio (any place you want—at home, in a park, in the school auditorium, you name it), you don't need fancy lighting, but you do need enough to show your grandchild clearly. For better picture quality, shoot with a camcorder instead of a camera or cell phone. The camera is good enough for your own computer and maybe a DVD, but if you want to post it publicly, you'll get better results from a camcorder.

Digital camcorders range from about $150 to over $3,500. At a store with knowledgeable staff, ask about the features you want. How high a resolution do you want for acceptable quality? How much zoom do you need: Will you be shooting from far away (like across a soccer field) or up close? Do you want a camcorder that uses a tape cassette, a mini DVD, a built-in hard drive, or a memory card? Check the size and weight to see which model fits your hand and is comfortable to use. Check the quality of the display in the store. For the best audio quality, you'll want a model that accepts an external microphone. If you'll be traveling with it, you'll want to consider a flash-memory or hard-drive-based model. Before you buy, research prices at several outlets and online, and then try to get the best price from your local store; you may need hands-on help down the line.

You can post your videos on your own website or blog, or on one of the many online video sites, many of which are free, including www.youtube.com. To post on YouTube, go to the site and click "Sign Up" and then "Create an Account." When your account is confirmed, click "Upload" and follow directions, which will include finding your video on your computer. You can also upload from your cell phone. The upload is limited to ten minutes and 1,024 megabytes (MB), which will take one to five minutes on a high-speed connection. You can either post publicly for the world to see or privately to keep it in the family. Either way, you'll have fun in the doing, the shooting, and the viewing.

Jog Together at Midnight

The first time I jogged with my grandson, Stefan, he was eight and I was fifty-seven. I had been running every morning for a dozen years, entering local road races, and sometimes even coming in first in my age group, a development that I, a non-athlete all my life, have never ceased to be amazed by. Stefan challenged me to a race, and to no one's surprise, he beat me handily, and then said, "I don't know how you got all those prizes (trophies I had won in age categories), you're not fast!" I told him, "I race against other old ladies."

Whether it was that victory over this more experienced (albeit creakier) runner that inspired him to greater lengths I don't know. I do know that he continued to run in the hills around his home; that, as a teenager, he entered and finished a triathlon involving running, biking, and swimming (with no preparation for the event, which horrified me, but that's the difference between young muscles and those of greater longevity); and that one of the high points in my career as a grandmother, and as a runner, came when the two of us ran the four-mile (6.4-kilometer) New Year's Eve Midnight Run in New York's Central Park sponsored by the New York Road Runners Club (www.nyrrc.org).

Stefan, his grandfather, and I drove into Manhattan for an early light dinner and a movie and then made our way to Central Park. As we walked into the park, we could hear loud rock music, and when I could see Stefan keeping time to the beat, I could tell he felt he was in the right place. We hung around the bandstand, danced a little, rattled our noisemakers, and then lined up to see the costume parade, which gets more outrageous every year. At the stroke of midnight, fireworks exploded in the Manhattan sky, and the race was on. Grandpa (not a runner) stayed to watch and take photos, and Stefan and I moved along with the throng. He slowed his pace so that I could keep up with him, and we stopped every now and then at the champagne stops along the course, which replaced the usual race-course water stops.

From time to time, he would look at me and grin and say, "I can't believe I'm doing this with my grandmother!" For years, this race has been my favorite way of celebrating New Year's, and sharing it with Stefan made it the best ever. Every time I wear the T-shirt we received that night, I treasure the memory of that special experience.

SHARING A SPORT

Whatever your sport is, it's fun to share it with your grandchildren. Sometimes the sharing just involves going to all the grandchildren's games, as Lou did with her eight grandchildren, who were all involved in sports of one kind or another throughout their school days, and four received sports scholarships to college.

Other grandmothers end up as coaches, as Valara has with her eleven-year-old granddaughter BréAwna's Elite Saints All-Stars cheerleading squad in Houston, Texas. (For the top 100 cheerleading sites in the United States and Canada, go to www.leaguelineup.com/topsites.asp?url=sacheerleading&sid

=722174762.) In a parents' cheerleading exhibition, Valara wore black leggings, a yellow T-shirt, and a rhinestone-studded bandanna, as she strutted her own stuff doing splits, cartwheels, and lifts. Says BréAwna, "I know she understands what it's like to be on the mat in front of everybody." And Valara says, "It was exhausting! I'm an old lady reliving my youth." This is how the grandchildren keep us young, or make us young again!

Publish a Family Cookbook

*E*dith had always loved to cook, and after she retired from teaching, she decided to get all her recipes together in an organized form. The project turned out to be bigger than she had anticipated, and ended up involving her three children and eight grandchildren, and resulting in *The Warner Family and Friends' Cookbook.*

Edith's daughter found the website **www.familycookbook project.com** (started by a grandfather who made his own cookbook and then won an award for the best online cookbook site). Edith registered on the site and proceeded to collect 222 recipes from family and friends. The one that has garnered the most hits online is Edith's sixteen-year-old granddaughter Lauren's "Chex Mix Puppy Chow," a snack that should tickle every child with a sweet tooth. To get the recipe, go to the website and search for "puppy chow."

Edith and her family worked on the cookbook for about eight months, and found putting in color photos (including one of all eight grandchildren) and personal comments among the most enjoyable parts. "It's been a wonderful experience," she says. (If I do this project, I'll have to include seven-year-old Nina's recipe for "chickin soup," using "1 cup of carits, 1 lb. of chickin, 2 cups of newtuls, 2 cups of tumaytoaw joos, and 1 cup of selury.")

PRODUCING YOUR OWN COOKBOOK

- Set a deadline. Edith went on the site in February, and in April set a deadline for October. Periodic reminders went out to family members who had not yet responded.
- Allow time to edit the recipes and to catch typos, misspellings, and errors, which creep in like gremlins.
- Go to the "Process" page on **www.familycookbookproject. com**, for helpful directions.
- Suggest that contributors assemble all ingredients in order at the beginning of the recipes so that entries will be uniform.
- Registration on the site costs $29.95 a year for an unlimited number of contributors and unlimited number of recipes; $19.95 for up to 100 recipes from up to ten contributors; and a thirty-day free trial.
- You need to order a minimum of fifty books, the cost of which varies according to the number of recipes and color photos and a couple of other options. Cost per book for Edith's 170-page book was $9 each.
- To explore other websites, go to **www.google.com** and search for "family cookbooks."

Going Places with Teen Grandchildren

When Harriet and her husband took their fifteen-year-old grandchildren to Alaska from their home in Minnesota, she was prepared for the twins to hate the formal dinner night on their four-day cruise. But both Haley and John were excited to dress up, Haley in a black sleeveless dress with a lace shawl and John in blazer, white shirt, and tie. Before dinner, John announced, "Grandma, I'm going to be adventurous and order different things from the menu," and he ordered duck for the first time. Harriet framed the ship photographer's photo of the kids in their formal attire and gave it to the children's father for his birthday. (Tragically, the twins' mother had recently died in a car crash; one reason for the trip was to give everyone a respite from grief.)

Haley took her own photos too, about 1,800 digital pictures, one of which, of Mount McKinley, won a prize at the Olmsted County Fair. The twins' other highlights included seeing whales, panning for gold (during the land portion of the trip), seeing a lumberjack show, and taking the bus tour in Denali Park.

Intergenerational travel is one of the fastest-growing trends in the world of travel and leisure, and teenagers (who may be underwhelmed by the idea of traveling with their parents) often love to go with grandparents. Why not? Who else would be so indulgent! Such trips build lifelong memories of shared good times.

RECIPE FOR A SUCCESSFUL TRIP

Preparation is the key for making the most of a shared journey with grandchildren of any age, and Harriet seems to have thought of everything. She typed a list of clothes the twins would need, emphasizing layering ("dress like an onion" is always good advice), formal clothes, and raingear. She obtained a notarized letter from the twins' father, giving them permission to travel with their grandparents. Each teen carried a personal packet with itinerary, airline tickets, meal vouchers, and information about Alaska. When Harriet learned of a TV show about Alaska, she called the youngsters to watch it.

Technology helped, first in trip planning, as they all logged on together to government websites and downloaded information on passport requirements and security procedures. On the trip itself, John brought his mother's laptop computer, Haley her digital camera, and both called their father several times on their cell phone.

It's important for grandparents to talk ahead of time to children's parents, first to get permission to take the children, and then for vital info on allergies, food preferences, and special interests, and tips on working with each child's unique personality. Most grandparents find it best to take only one or two grandchildren at a time, often when they reach a certain age.

My friend Silvia has taken each of her granddaughters, one at a time, to London for a week, and learned why you shouldn't read kids' diaries, when she peeked and read in one teen's diary: "I saw a sweater I liked, but Nana was too cheap to buy it for me." The girl never breathed a word of this to Nana, Silvia kept her sense of humor, and they both enjoyed the trip.

Grandma's Quilting Camp

Betty liked her Texas friend's idea of taking grandchildren camping, except for one little thing: Betty wasn't a camper. Undaunted, she developed her own idea of using the "camp" image of shared fun to change an ordinary visit to Grandma's house to a special memory.

With 13 grandchildren of various ages, Betty developed different activities for all of them, focusing on "camping" with one or two children at a time, ranging from baking to beach to golf. As a quilter for 42 years and the Michigan-based publisher of quilting books (**www.qbu.com**), Betty saw quilting as a natural "camp" activity, especially when fourteen-year-old Sarah became interested in making a lap-size quilt for a wounded soldier through the nationwide program Quilts of Valor (**www.qovf.org**).

Betty had taught her grandchildren the rudiments of sewing, sometimes piecing squares together to make pillowcases. Now she and Sarah worked together on their quilt. Sarah knew the pattern she wanted: red, white, and blue, with stars and a flag. They went through several books, Sarah found her flag pattern, and Betty showed her a design of a five-pointed star from one of her own books. They did the math and design work together, and the next morning Sarah found the blue fabric she wanted for her fields of stars.

With the use of rotary-cutting methods, Betty and Sarah cut, sewed, and pressed, working back and forth. The relatively easy design made the work go quickly, so Sarah could finish sewing the top together in just two days. After Betty saw a story in the local paper about a serviceman returning from Iraq who had received a Purple Heart for his bravery and his wounds, she and Sarah arranged to present their quilt to him. He and his wife were touched by a young person's concern and expressed their thanks for the beautiful quilt. To Betty, a quilt is symbolic of warmth, comfort, and care. "It's our way of saying 'thank you,'" she says.

QUILTING TOGETHER

Says Sarah, "This was a once-in-a-lifetime experience." The quilt-making process was a time of bonding, as Sarah enjoyed her conversations with Grandma Betty and found out how far quilting has taken Betty in her life. Sarah also said how much fun she had, how proud she was of making the quilt—and "Whew! What a relief it was when it was done!"

"Anyone who sews can make a quilt by piecing shapes together," says Betty. The key here is "anyone who sews"! If you have not sewn before, you need to practice using the sewing machine. To learn straight stitching, practice with a striped or plaid fabric. Modern rotary cutting tools (a round blade like a pizza-cutter that cuts through fabric on a mat made especially for cutting on) make the process go quicker, but scissors and rulers still work as they did in years past. You may find a class in quilting at a local fabric or sewing machine store. The Quilts of

Valor program can arrange to have a quilt top finished off, so you don't have to do the actual quilting yourself. The website www.qovf.org also offers suggestions for participants.

Helpful books include the "Turning Twenty" series, by Tricia Cribbs, which specialize in unique easy designs, and *The Giving Quilt,* by Kathy Cueva and Susan Zeigler (both available from www.qbu.com).

Resources

|||||||||||||||||||||||||||||||||||||||||

Y ou don't have to be computer-literate to be a cool grand-mother, but once you start moving around in cyber-space, you'll wonder how you ever got along just rambling around on Earth. If you're not comfortable using a computer, check out your local adult education programs or public library, and you're sure to find introductory classes. Or you can always ask a grandchild to get you started. She or he will love the chance to teach you for a change.

The websites below are an idiosyncratic collection. Some I learned about from the grandmothers whose stories are in this book. Some I use regularly for everything from travel to recipes to finding books and movies. They're all accurate at the time of this writing, but whether they'll stay that way is anybody's guess. If any of these are no longer on the Internet, a gazillion others will pop up to take their place. To find a website about any topic, type what you want to find into a search engine and you'll come up with enough websites to keep you at your computer for the rest of your life.

ALL ABOUT ME

- My website: www.SallyWendkosOlds.com
- My blog: Super Granny, at http://omasally.blogspot.com

- My daughter's website (she designed my website and lots of others): www.dorriolds.com

INFORMATION, PLEASE

- You can find an amazing world of information with these search engines: My favorite is www.google.com. Other people swear by www.ask.com, www.yahoo.com, www.HotBot.com, www.AltaVista.com, www.Lycos.com, and probably by the time this is published, there will be more. Try one or more and see which one you like best.
- For a brief encyclopedia-type entry about anything, anyplace, or anybody: www.wikipedia.com. (Anyone can post or edit an entry, so take the information with a grain of salt.)
- Information on this day in history: www.scopesys.com/anyday, www.infoplease.com/dayinhistory, or http://memory.loc.gov/ammem/today/today.html

JUST FOR GRANNIES (AND GRANDPAS TOO)

- A wealth of grandparent-related information: www.grandparents.com
- AARP (American Association of Retired People) Grandparent Information Center: www.AARP.org
- Foundation for Grandparenting, a website that focuses on research, education, programs, and communication about grandparenting: www.grandparenting.org
- Information and events for Grandparents' Day: http://grandparents-day.com

- Resources for Canadian grandparents: www.todaysgrand-parent.com
- National Committee of Grandparents for Children's Rights (NCGCR), for state laws about grandparent visitation and custody: www.grandparentsforchildren.org
- Administration on Aging—issues involving three generations of grandparents raising grandchildren: www.aoa.gov/prof/notes/notes_grandparents.asp
- Information for grandparents raising grandchildren: Generations United: www.GU.org and www.grandfactsheets.org/state_fact_sheets.cfm. (Also, search for "grandparents raising grandchildren.")
- Miscellaneous articles about relationships, activities, etc.: http://yourlifeafter50.com/category/grandparenting, *Grand Magazine:* www.grandmagazine.com/, and *Modern Senior Living Magazine:* www.seniorlvgmag.com
- Senior Living: http://seniorliving.about.com/od/family matters/
- The Association of Grandparents of Indian Immigrants: www.agiivideo.com
- Jewish grandparents: www.myjewishlearning.com/daily_life/relationships/TO_Parent_Child/Grandparenting.htm?gclid=CPbz0cmA4Z QCFQObFQod6lz_QA
- Christian grandparents: www.christianitytoday.com/par enting/features/expert/grandparents.html
- Grandparents' University at Michigan State University: www.grandparents.msu.edu
- Grandparents' University at the University of Wyoming: www.uwalumni.com/grandparents

BUYING STUFF

- Online retailer of books and other bookstore-type items: www.barnesandnoble.com
- Online retailers of books and any other products you can think of: www.amazon.com
- Inexpensive gifts for grandchildren: http://happybirds craftinghaven.blogspot.com
- Good ideas for gifts, searchable by grandkids' ages, gender, and type of gift (active, board game, computer, etc.) and even gifts for moms and grannies: www.grandkidsgift guide.com

COMMUNICATING WITH GRANDKIDS

- To set up a free or cheap phone and webcam program: www.skype.com or www.Jajah.com
- Information, books, and products about baby signing gestures: www.signingbaby.com
- The most common terms and phrases in texting and emails: www.TechDictionary.com
- Teen abbreviations: www.teenchatdecoder.com/parental lookup/teenchat-a.html
- Shorthand for emailing and text messaging: www.netlingo.com/emailsh.cfm
- Teen lingo (with a warning about offensive terms): www.thesource4ym.com/teenlingo/
- Email stationery: www.thundercloud.net

CRAFTS

- Company that makes tableware from kids' artwork: www.makit.com
- Gingerbread house kits: www.wilton.com
- Finger-knitting instructions: www.knitty.com/issue summer06/FEATfingerknitting.html, www.youtube.com/watch?v=xMQr_nLn4FM, and www.kyledesigns.com/product/FINGER-KNITTING
- Kids' knitting needles and information on teaching kids to knit: www.morehousefarm.com/GiftIdeas/Children/, www.purplekittyyarns.com/index.asp?PageAction=VIEW PROD&ProdID=137, and http://pages.eyarn.com/6030/PictPage/1922208403.html
- Teaching kids to crochet: http://kniting.thecrochettips.com/index.php/59/crochet-for-beginners/
- Quilting directions: www.lucyfazely.com/howto/piecetop.htm
- Publisher and seller of books about quilting: www.qbu.com
- Quilts of Valor, to make lap quilts for wounded soldiers: www.qovf.org
- Producing a family cookbook: www.familycookbookproject.com
- Free beginner quilt patterns: http://freequilt.com

BEING CYBER-SAVVY

- Working with digital photos: printing them and putting them into books and other products: www.shutterfly.com and www.kodakgallery.com

- Computer education and use for seniors: www.seniornet.com
- Line drawings you can print for your grandchild to color: www.preschoolcoloringbook.com/color/
- To create a free blog, complete with directions: www.blogger.com or http://wordpress.org
- To upload your own videos: www.YouTube.com, www.blip.tv.com, www.dailymotion.com, www.veoh.com, www.googlevideo.com, www.aol.com, www.yahoovideo.com, and www.myspace.com

GARDENING

- Gardening with children: www.kidsgardening.com, www.eartheasy.com/grow_gardening_children.htm, and www.urbanext.uiuc.edu/firstgarden
- Advice on using hypertufa: www.efildoog-nz.com and www.backyardgardener.com

GRANDMOTHER BLOGS

- Super Granny: http://OmaSally.blogspot.com
- Nourishing Relationships: http://nourishingrelationships.blogspot.com/
- Grandma's Corner: www.ninalewis.com
- Play Wit Me Nana: http://playwitmenana.blogspot.com
- Musings on a Lazy Afternoon: http://margaret.theworths.org
- Nana's Corner: http://nanascorner.com
- Grandma Henke: http://grandmahenke.com/grandma
- Boondock Babble: http://boondockbabble.blogspot.com

- From Mom to Grandma: www.momtograndma.com
- One Happy Bird: www.happybirdscraftinghaven.com/

KIDS' HEALTH AND SAFETY

- A wealth of information: www.keepkidshealthy.com. (Among its valuable help is the number to call if you think a child has swallowed something poisonous: 1-800-222-1222—and post this where you can find it in a hurry—kids swallow the darndest things.)
- Emergency treatment for a child with a history of allergies: www.EpiPen.com
- National Program for Playground Safety: www.uni.edu/playground/
- Health and safety information for kids and teens: www.kidshealth.org

MUSIC

- Kids' songs: www.BusSongs.com or www.kididdles.com/lyrics
- Folksongs: www.mudcat.org. (This one also gives instructions for making your own musical instruments.)
- Popular (or popular when you were young) love songs: www.romantic-lyrics.com

SHARING YOURSELF

- The Legacy Project, an educational, intergenerational project that offers free online activities and guides, books, essay contests, and community programs, all about connecting to what matters in your past, present, and future at any age: www.legacyproject.org

- A grandparents' page that helps orient you to everything on the site: www.legacyproject.org/grandparents.html
- For a downloadable form that helps you share your life information with your grandchild: www.legacyproject.org/holidaykit/part2/hd2.5lifestory. html
- A Life Statement Library lets you record a personal Life Statement, to pass on your values to your grandchildren: www.legacyproject.org/programs/lifestatements.html

SPORTS

- New York Road Runners Club: www.nyrrc.org
- Top 100 cheerleading sites in the United States and Canada: www.leaguelineup.com/topsites.asp?url=sacheer leading&sid=722174762
- Advice for taking kids skiing: www.momsteam.com

TRAVEL

- Travel info, outdoor tips, and product info: www.funtravels.com
- Travel newsletter—ask for a free sample issue: www.intltravelnews.com
- Educational travel experiences: www.elderhostel.org/programs
- Company that offers small-group travel experiences: www.generationstouringcompany.com
- Information on visiting New York City: www.nycvisit.com

- River-rafting company: www.RaftIdaho.com
- Segway tours: www.citysegwaytours.com
- For ideas on family farm visits:
  www.familytravelguides.com/articles/farms/kidfarm1.html
  www.familytravelguides.com/articles/farms/kidfarm2.html

BETTERING THE WORLD

- Nonprofit Christian organization that helps orphans and leads missions: www.horizoninternationalinc.com
- Grandmothers' peace activist group:
  www.grandmothersforpeace.org/gatw

Acknowledgments

|||||||||||||||||||||||||||||||||||||||||||

s every writer knows, you don't do it all by yourself. There are always other people who give you a helping hand all along the way to publication.

First I want to thank the Super Grannies who shared with me their stories about what they do or did with their grandchildren. Some of these wonderful women are close friends of mine, some are in my family, some are classmates from the best public school in Philadelphia—the Philadelphia High School for Girls—some are my ever-helpful colleagues in the American Society of Journalists and Authors, and some were strangers when I first contacted them who became friends as they let me into their families' lives.

I also want to thank those grannies who wrote to me at my blog and who inspired me with theirs. And of course I want to thank the one grandpa who appears in these pages because I just couldn't leave him out.

Special thanks are due my professional guides—Linda Konner, my terrific agent, who believed in the book right from the first germ of the idea; Jennifer Williams, my responsive editor, whose constant enthusiasm kept me buoyant; and Rodman Neumann, my project editor, who smoothly shepherded the book through production and who never said no to any of my requests.

And of course, I give extravagant thanks to the most important people connected to this book and to me—my beloved family. My husband and best friend, David Mark Olds, read every word in manuscript form and made suggestions that made the book better. My marvelous and accomplished older daughters, Nancy Olds and Jennifer Möbus, made me a grandmother in the first place, gave me the gift of getting to know their amazing children, and followed the book's progress with interest and ideas. My equally marvelous and accomplished youngest daughter, Dorri Olds, "mom" to grand-dog Buddy, often interrupted her own busy work days to give me technical and artistic help. And my incomparable grandchildren, Stefan, Maika, Anna, Lisa, and Nina, have given me countless interesting and joyous hours.

Index

Preschool years (age 3 to 6), xviii, 47–48
Presents, shopping for. *See* Shopping

Quilting
    adding culture and traditions to, 3–5
    Grandma's Quilting Camp, 200–202
    as intergenerational activity, 164–165

Reading activities. *See* Books
Recollections/reflections
    on adolescence, 175–176
    on author's grandmother, xv
    of grandmother's workplace, 95–97
    on infancy to age 3, 1–2
    on preschool ears, 47–48
    on school years, 99–100
Religion. *See* Traditions
Resources
    author's collection of websites, 203–211
    computer communications, 16–17
    creating books, 42
    creating cookbooks, 197
    family blog, 184
    games for babies, 19
    gardening, 137–138
    knitting directions, 74
    Make-A-Plate kits, 65
    making a birth book, 8
    for music, 14
    outdoor travels, 63
    poetry for children, 34
    quilting, 5, 202
    for religious traditions, 152

for Segway tours, 187
text messaging, 182
for using hypertufa, 145
using this book for, xviii–xix
on values and beliefs, 154–155
Rules
    age-appropriate, 109–111
    grandparent privileges with, 57–58
    traveling with children, 199

Safety rules
    for adventure travel, 131–132
    for international travel, 189
    Internet resources, 209
    with knitting needles, 73
    for sports activities, 150
School years (age 6 to 11), xviii, 99–100
Scrapbooking, 6–8
Sewing, 164–165. *See also* Knitting; Quilting
Shopping
    for costume parties, 60
    excursions for children, 156–158
    Internet resources, 206
    never being in rush for, 39
    for presents, 79–81
Signing/sign language, 20–22
Singing. *See* Music
Sports. *See also* Physical fitness
    baseball, 66–67
    cheerleading, 194–195
    with grandchildren, 194–195
    Internet resources, 210
    jogging/running, 193–194
    newspaper basketball, 75
    skiing, 149–150
Teaching
    appreciation for music, 139–140, 146–148

The Granny Who Wrote This Book

SALLY WENDKOS OLDS loves to keep the Wendkos in her name, because every Wendkos in the world is a relative of hers. She has one husband, David Mark Olds, sometimes known as David, sometimes as Mark. She has three daughters, Nancy, Jennifer, and Dorri; one grandson, Stefan; four granddaughters, Maika, Anna, Lisa, and Nina; and one grand-dog, Buddy. She also has honorary children and grandchildren in the form of five nephews, two nieces, six great-nieces, and three great-nephews, most of whom are Wendkoses. She has written eleven books, counting this one; more than 200 articles; a handful of poems; and more emails than she could possibly count. To learn more about Sally, go to her website: **www.SallyWendkosOlds.com** and her blog: **http://omasally.blogspot.com**. She would love to hear from grandmothers, grandchildren, grandfathers, and anyone else who feels moved to write. Send emails to **WendkosOlds @alumni.upenn.edu** or postal letters c/o Sterling Publishing Co., Inc., 387 Park Avenue South, New York, NY 10016-8810.